FLIGHT

VOLUME FIVE

Michel Gagné's

The Saga of Rex

"the broken path"

FLIGHT
VOLUME FIVE

V

Villard • New York

Flight: Volume Five is a work of fiction. Names, places, and incidents either are a product of the authors' imaginations or are used fictiously. Any resemblance to actual events, locales, or persons, living or dead, is entirely coincidental.

2008 Villard Books Trade Paperback Edition

Published in the United States by Villard Books, an imprint of The Random House Publishing Group, a division of Random House, Inc., New York.

VILLARD and "V" CIRCLED Design are registered trademarks of Random House, Inc.

Published by arrangement with Flight Comics LLC.

ISBN 978-0-345-50589-7

Printed in the United States of America

www.villardbooks.com

2 4 6 8 9 7 5 3 1

Illustration on pages ii–iii by Reagan Lodge

Editor/Art Director: Kazu Kibuishi
Assistant Editors: Kean Soo and Phil Craven
Associate: Alfred Moscala
Our Editor at Villard: Chris Schluep

CONTENTS

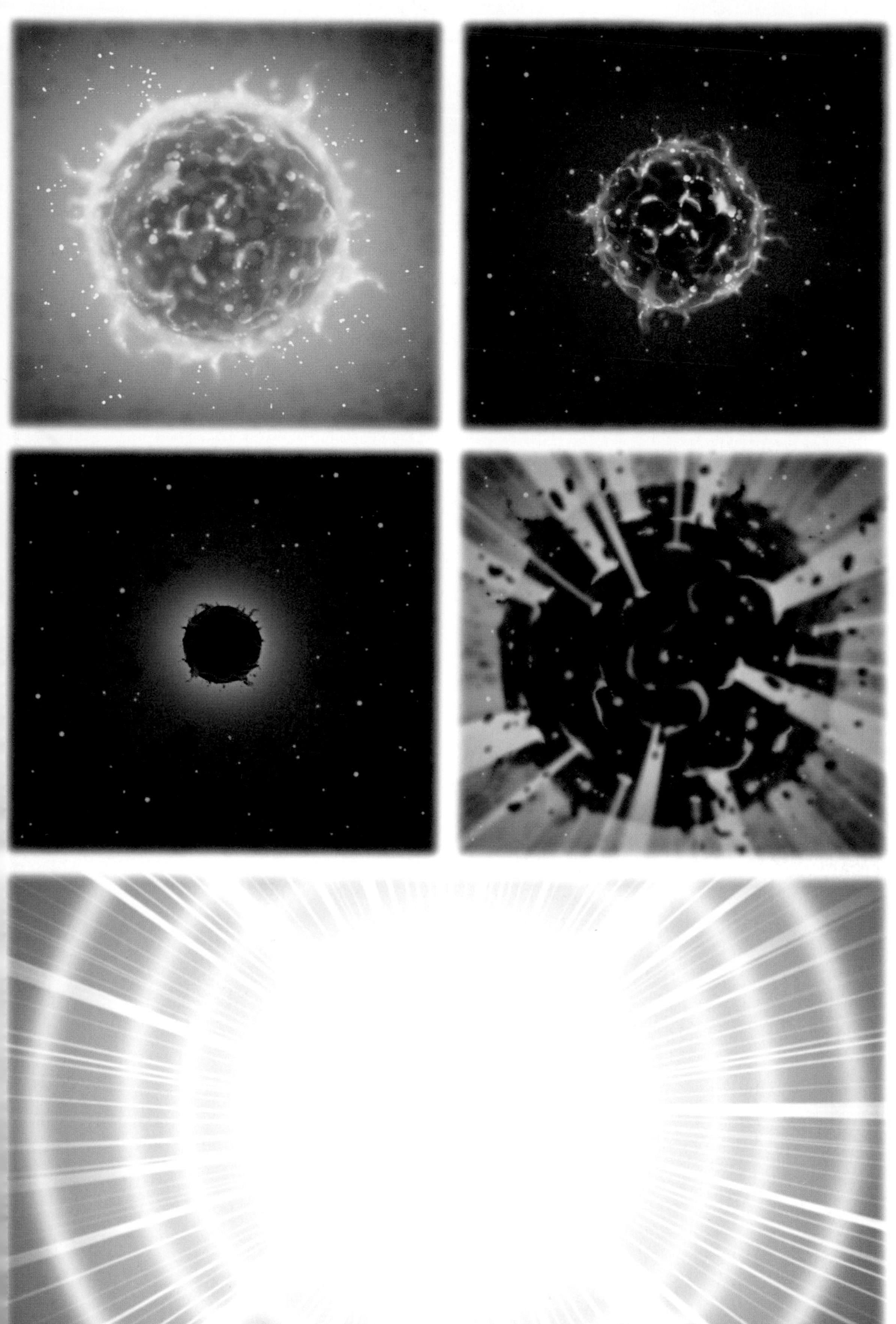

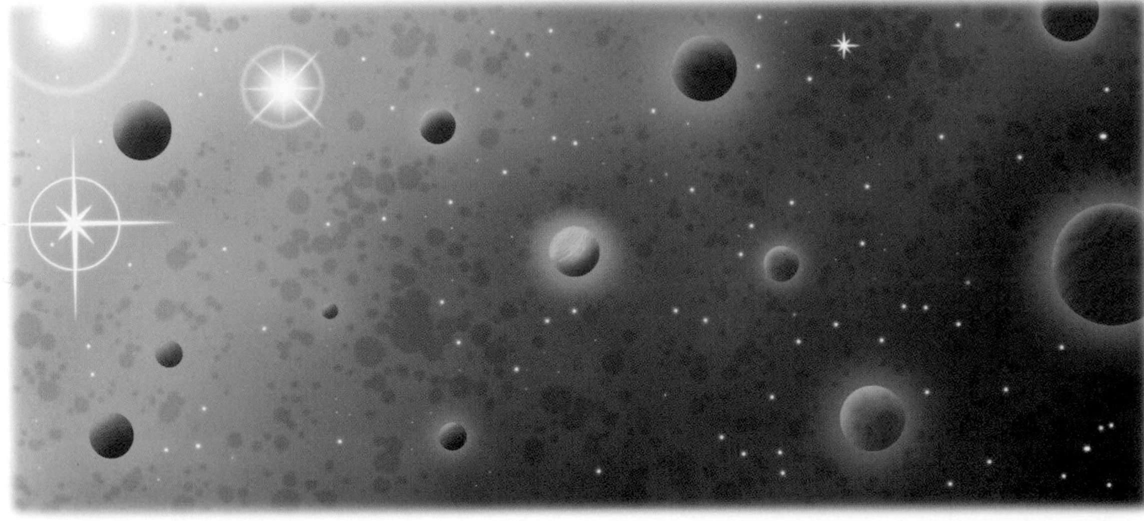

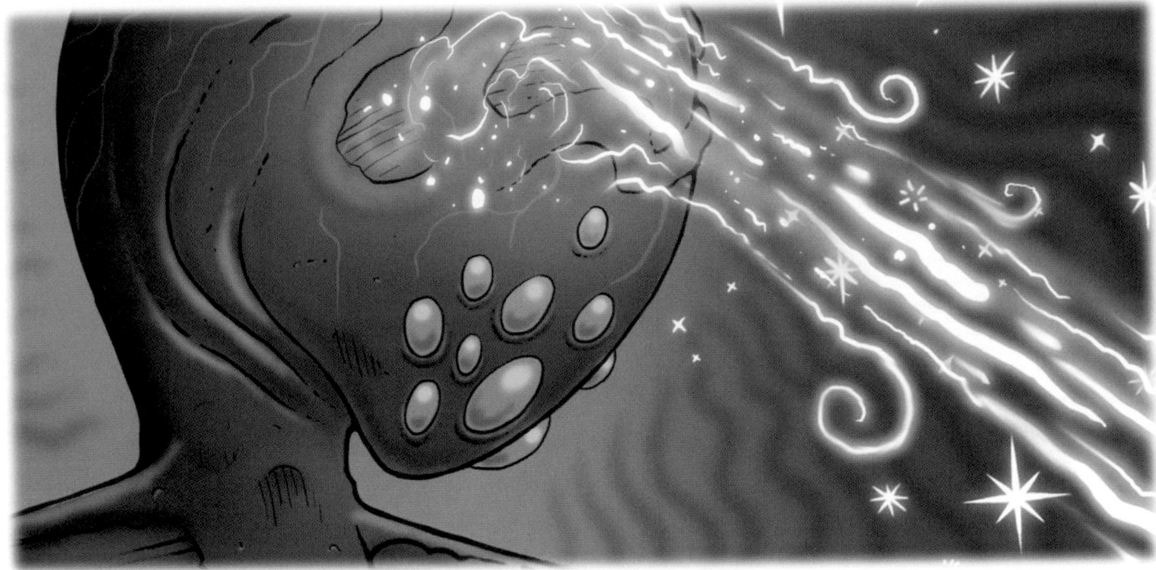

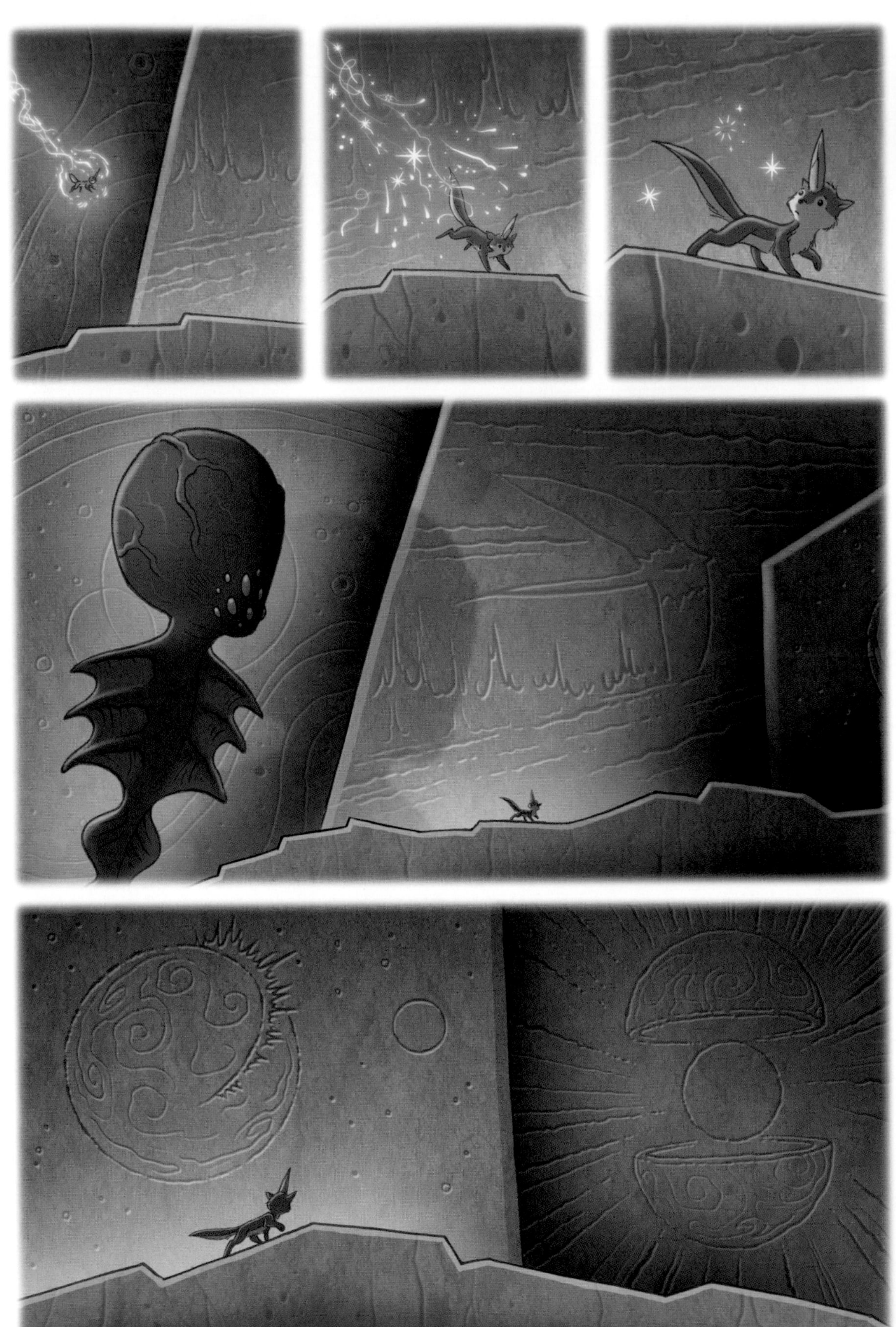

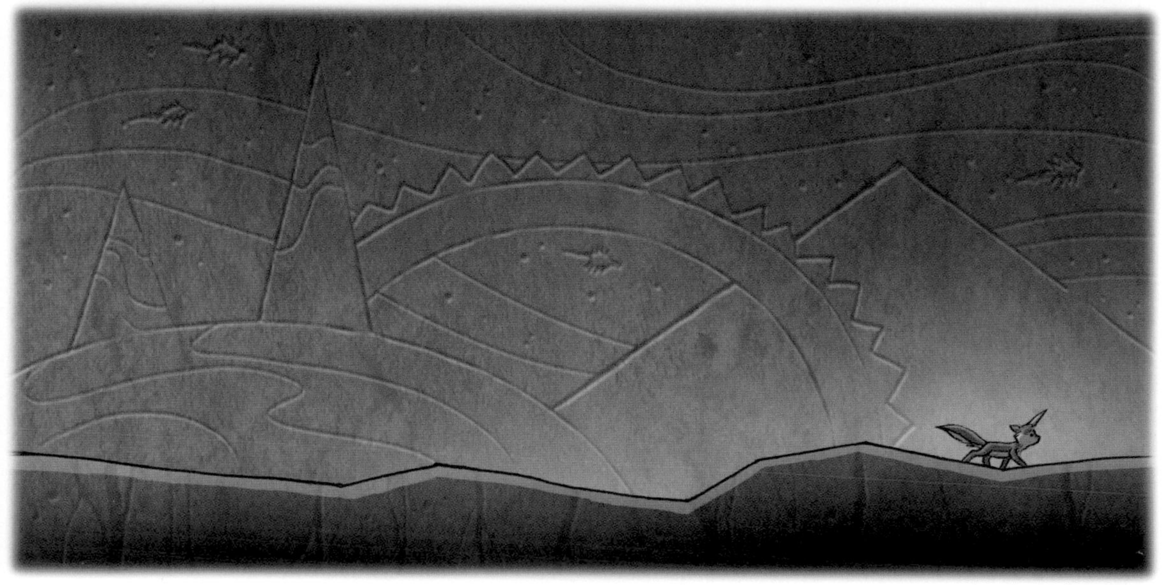

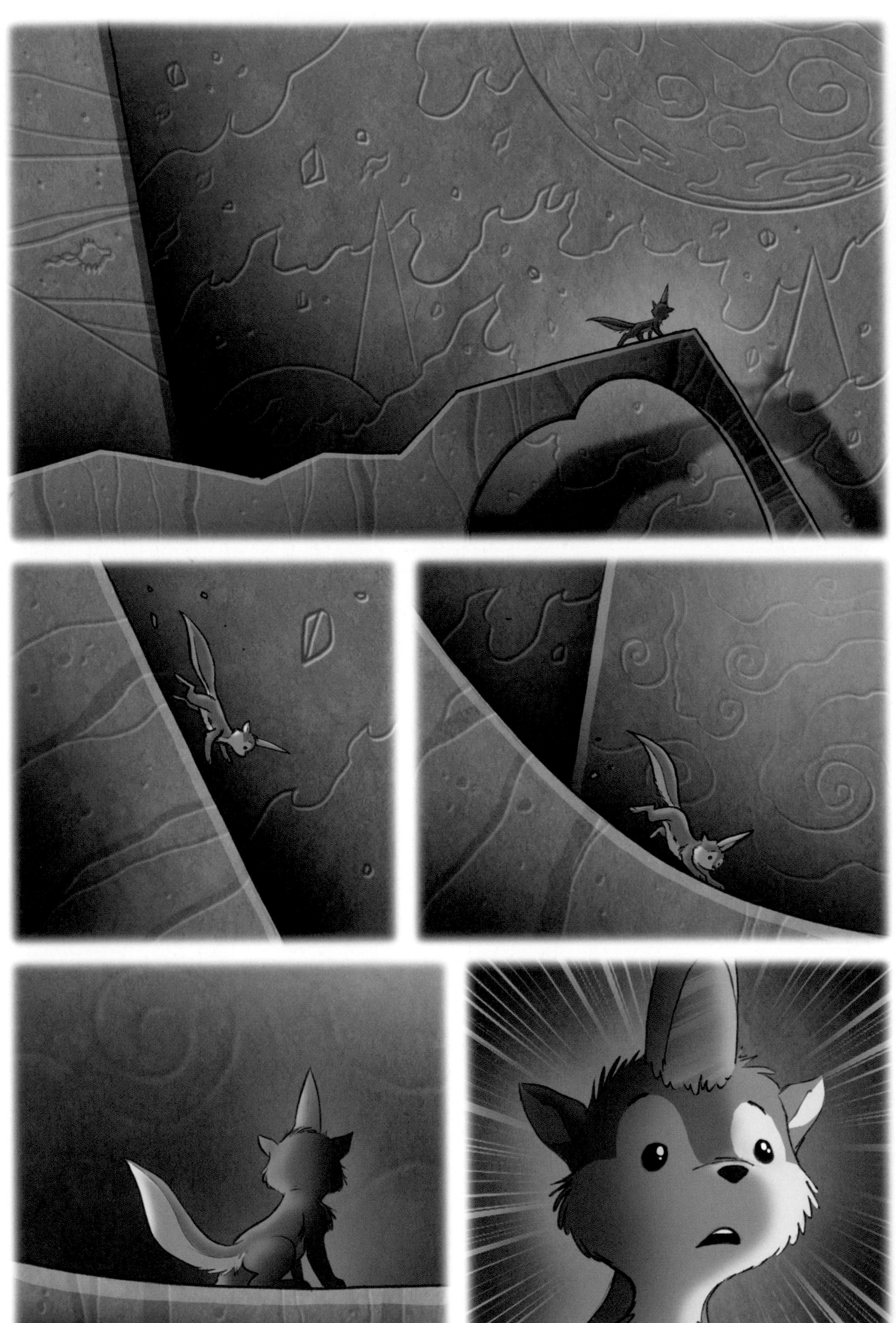

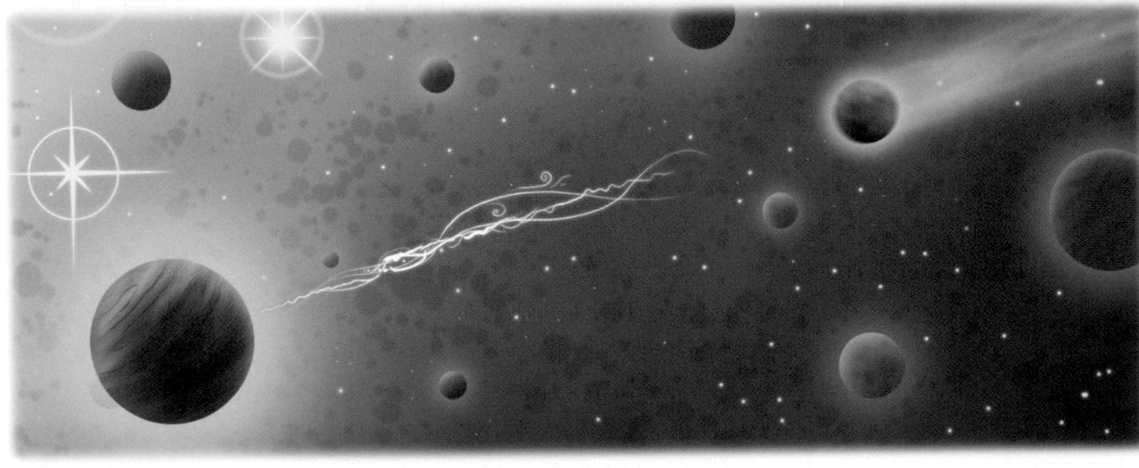

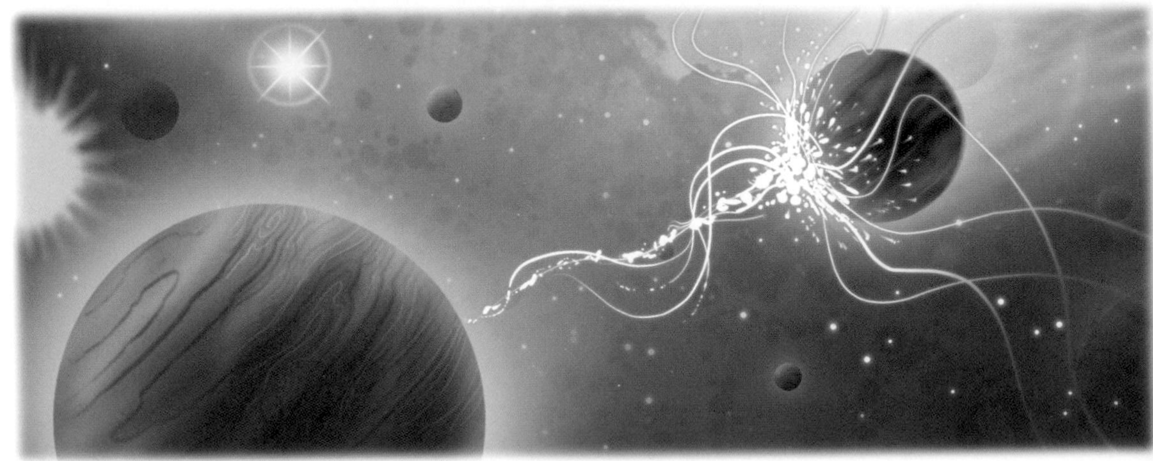

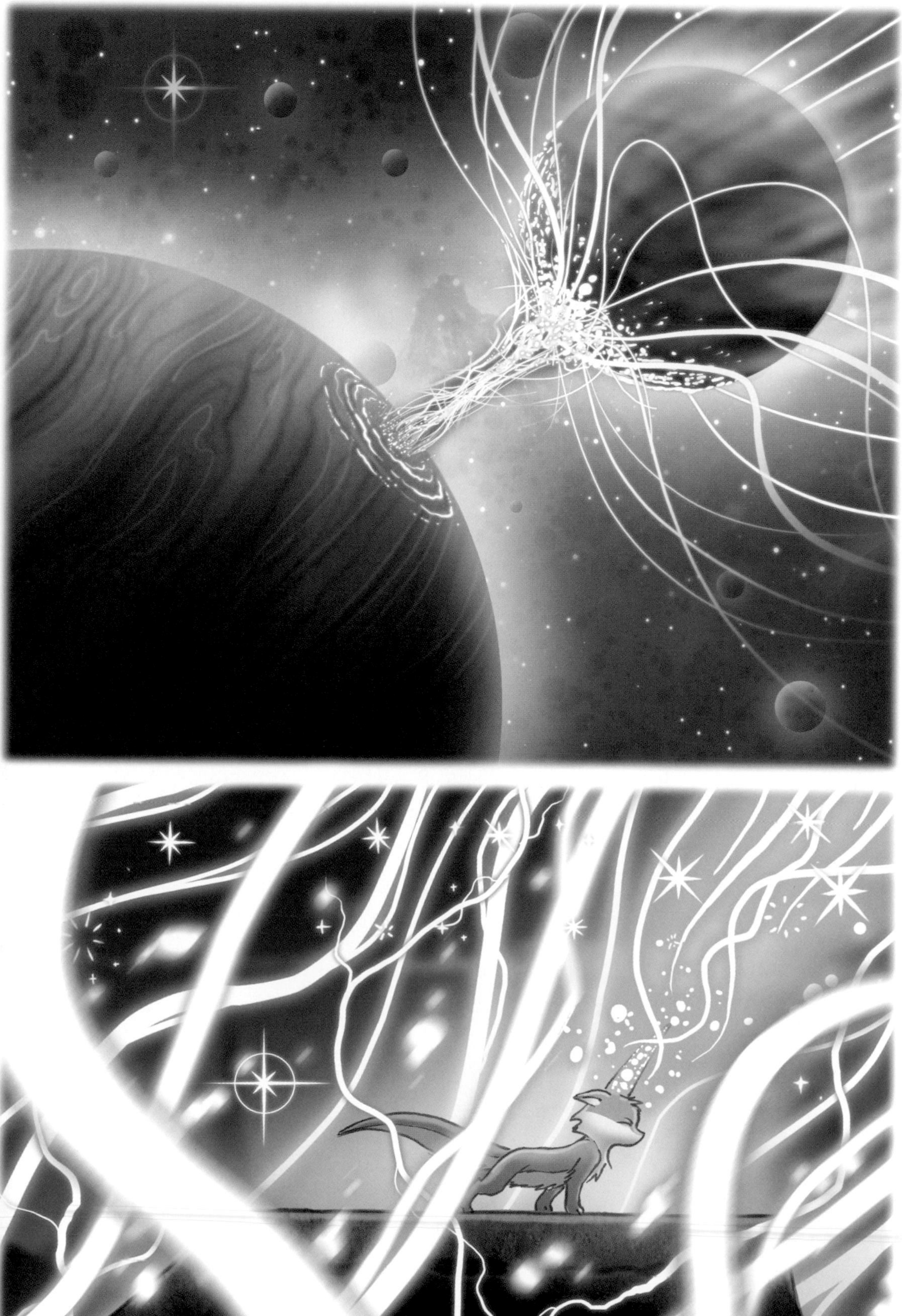

To be continued...

Delilah Dirk,
International Mistress of Swordsmanship

is greatly tested in

THE AQUEDUCT

A TALE OF ADVENTURE AND PERIL

told in a series of illustrated plates by

Tony Cliff, R.A.

LONDON, R.G. BARGIE, 80 THREADNEEDLE STREET.
PUBLISHED IN ORDINARY TO HER MAJESTY.
MMVII

My name is Selim Abd-Al Rahim. I am travelling companion to the illustrious Ms. Delilah Dirk, aboard her ship *Amphinome*.

I am not, however, permitted above-decks, as Ms. Dirk has determined that the pace of business in the cockpit exceeds that of my reactionary capacities.

So I occupy myself by examining a hold's worth of Ms. Dirk's recent acquisitions during this slow, uneventful voyage.

THUNK

DAMN IT!!

Perhaps not so uneventful?

Mr. Selim, please join me in the cockpit.

We have a problem.

Burning arrows.
Needless to say, not a ship captain's best friend.

What do we do?
I'll think of something!
I've been in worse situations.
Really?
Maybe not.
PLUMMETTTTTTT
Okay, We're going to jump.
Jump?
Surely not!
What about the other options? Are there other options? I would like to come up with other options!
Yes, all right.
Let's sit down and brainstorm.
But... what about the cargo?
and... the fall!
We worry about the cargo later!
The fall... um...

Aim for a tree!

WHOOP!

SHOOMP

SKRUNCH

ugh

RUMMAGE
RUMMAGE
RUMMAGE

STUMBLE

AAAARRGHH!!

Everything we were carrying is ruined. The vases are smashed. The tapestries are consumed by fire. And the jewels are—I think—buried underneath it all.
This crown? Well... it's okay.
but...
but...

AAAAARRRGGHHHH!!

I worked so hard for those things! Now they're just charred lumps of scrap!

UGH!

WHUMP

I'm sorry, I forgot to ask. Are you all right?

Well, I have bruises! Bruises covering most of ... um ... *this* area. Though, to be honest, they're less bothersome than the cramps I had developed in the hold of your late airship.
You, though? You seem to have a few twigs in your hair.
blech
Never worse.

Hm.
So...
Where do you think we may be?

OPTION 1. Head ***Northwest***.

Walk along the valley for who-knows how long, eventually dying from starvation, lack of water, exposure, or an unpleasant combination of all three.

OPTION 2. Head ***Southeast***.

Spend two days walking back to Hadid, where we may acquire some reliable transportation if we can avoid being beheaded.

Let's climb ***the Aqueduct.***

It's a straight, flat path, and we'll have all the drinking water we need.

Additionally, by its very nature it *must* lead us to some sort of civilization.

Plans?
No.

MUNCH
MUNCH

Miss Dirk?
Mister Selim?

Have you decided on a plan?

AAAAAAHHH!!!

NO!

No, Mr. Selim. I have ***not*** come up with a plan!

AND YOU KNOW WHAT? I'M NOT **GOING** TO COME UP WITH A PLAN!

All our options are ***equally horrible!***

But we...

NO!

AAAAARRGGHH!!!

CHUNK!

Gasp!
The Evil Army of Sulamein the Irascible!

The hills to the West! The trees would provide cover!
Perhaps...
No...

No, they have horses. Quite a few of them.
They'd cut us off easily.

So we either wait here for a bloody death, or...
The Aqueduct?

Curse you, Delilah Dirk!

So?

Perhaps not such a bad idea?

We'll see,
Mr. Selim.

Hm.

The horses are
wheeling away.

They're heading
off west.

Ha!
POOM

ZZZZZ

CHOOM

Damn it.

WHAT THE HELL WAS THAT??

No wonder the... the *cavalry* left! They probably didn't want to end up buried in rubble!
Buried like *we're* going to be buried!

I *knew* this was a horrible idea.
I let you talk me into *this*?
At least down there we had a fighting chance.
Up here, we just *die*.

SSSSSSSSSSS

Such a
horrible plan.

POOM

SPLOOSH

:GASP:

You...

Thank you, Mr. Selim.
and...

I'm..
For before,
uh
I'm very...

Come on, we can get to the top now.

We can jump for this side.
POOM
No, wait.
Get down!
What?
Augh! No!
Let go of me!
CHAMB!!
Hold on!

COUGH!
HACK!
Are you all right?
WHAT??
Are you all.right?
sshh
Yes. I think so.
Good.
Get ready.

SSCHHIINNNGGG

GLACK!

PIFF!

CRACK!!

Well played, Mr. Selim.
PHEW

I think I may have misjudged you.
You're sharper in a pinch than I've given you credit for.

So.
What do you suggest for now?

Hm.
I hadn't really thought that far ahead.

Ah, well.
I'm sure we'll come up with something
The End

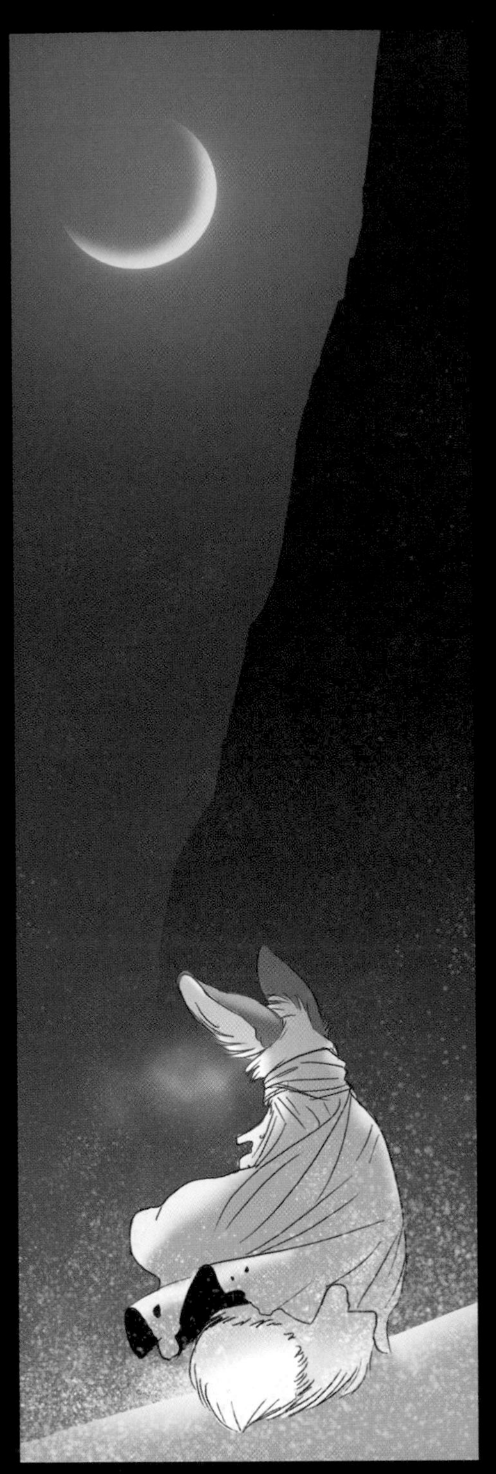

THE DRAGON

by

Reagan Lodge

Sweet yam! Only two coppers!

Thanks!

Wyit.

There's been a change in plans.
There's been heavy snow. I'll need to ride ahead to see if we'll be able to continue on through the mountains tonight.

Should I come too?

No.

I need you here until I'm back.

Until then, you will accompany Jin. He's offered to help our people through this region.

Keep an ear out for any news meanwhile. Remember that we're not in safe territory anymore. We need all the information we can get.

Hm. Look around then, shall we?
Your people drink tea?
Oh. Yeah. We do. You like tea too?
Quite. And we should see if anyone in town has some news of interest to Sidna.
Hmm?
Mmm, I did hear on the road that there's a teahouse in town...

It should be right around...
...Here?
Nice.
Must've closed a long time ago...
Hard times, these.
And I really wanted to try some new tea before we left.

How your leader expects us to find news in a frostbitten mining town so desolate as to not even have a teahouse is beyond me!
Watch it. We might be foreigners, but Sidna knows what she's doing.
FAH!
Well, any better ideas?
...Hey...

AACK!!
Wyit! RUN!!
WYIT!

sssss...OWWWW...

oh... my...

... God.

Oh God Oh God
Oh-
ACK!!
Ugh!!
Huh?

Jin!

Jin!! Where are y—

Sh.

What's happening?! What IS that thing?

A Dragon Tank.

I'll explain. Follow me!

So...
What now?

I've encountered armor like this before, yet this must be one of the newer models I've heard of. Type II steel plating, dual headguns, heavy lightning cannon, tri-core Z-type Amano engine... Highly advanced, but it seems to have some similarities to older models...

...And may have the same weakness.

...uh...

Didn't you see the size of that thing?! We need an army for this, not an arrow!

HAVE YOU A BETTER IDEA!?!

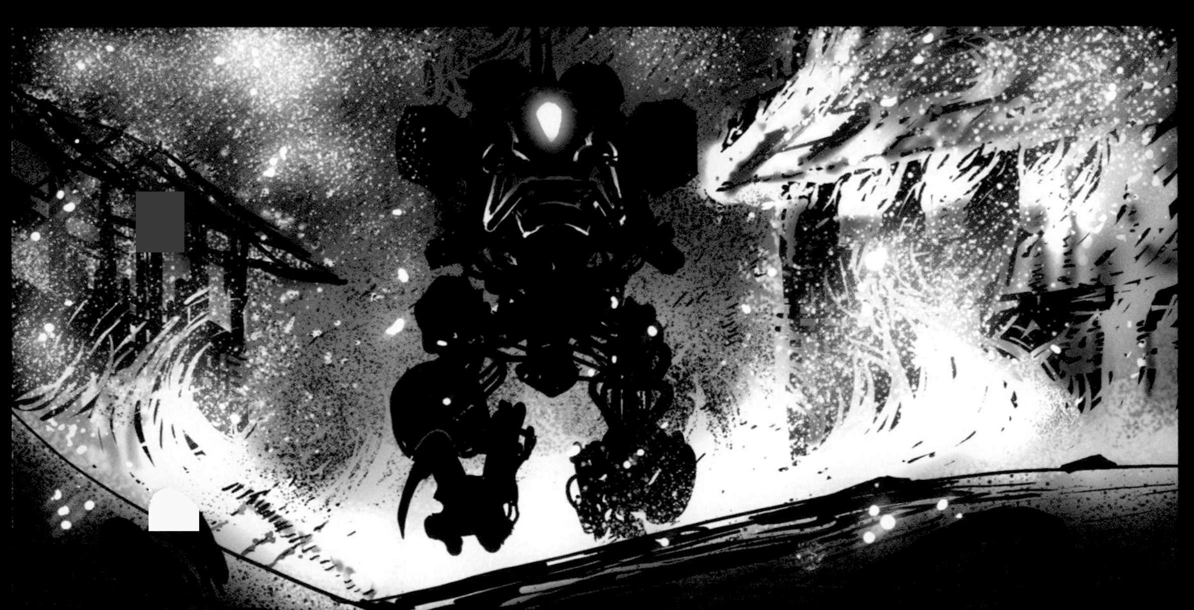

Come quickly now!

Is it...dead?
Quite dead.
I fear I made a terrible mistake in advising Sidna to pass through here.

Okay, wait.

NOW can you tell me what's going on? You said you'd explain.

Might as well...

Nothing more we can do for the town at this point. Everyone still alive would have fled by now.

That Dragon Tank was a Union model, no doubt about it. Yet even the Union wouldn't just destroy a neutral borderlands town without warning... unless it appeared as if the town were aiding your people and Sidna.

We should leave now. For all we know there could be more on the
JIN!

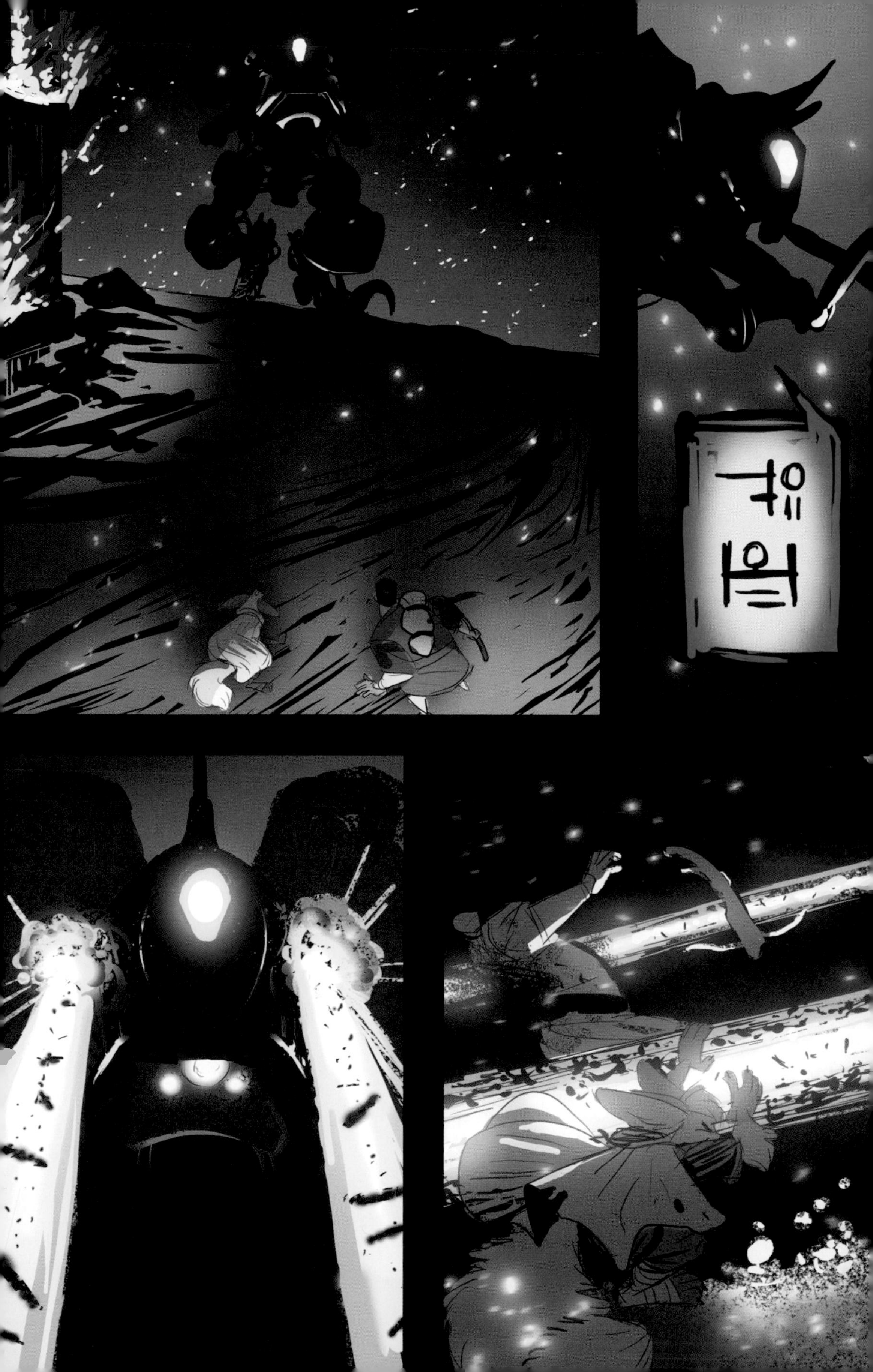

...ngh...
wy'it... run...
RUN!

Well then...

uh... HEY YOU!!

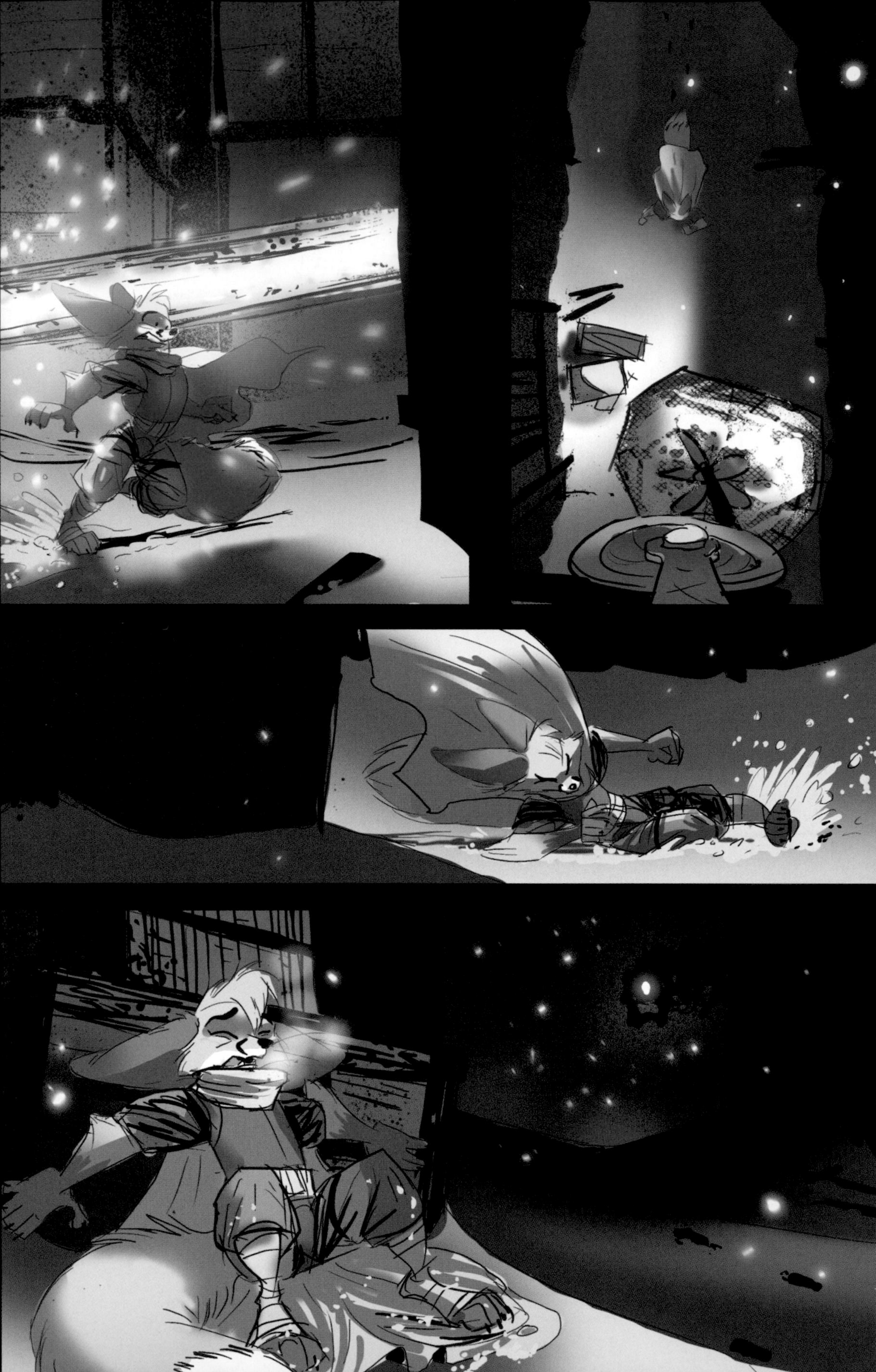

Damn.

NNNGH!!

Oof!

Oh GO TO HELL!!!

Just leave—
everyone
ALONE!
SHOOMP

Sidna-
Where are you?

Oh CRAP!!

AAGH!!!

등: 여

Wyit!
Wake up!
Come on!

The...the town...Sidna, it's gone, and...and Jin...
I know. I came back as soon as I could.
But we need to keep moving. Our people depend on us.
I know... I just want to leave this place.
I...I understand. Come, we'll go now.

You should try to get some rest. It's still a long way back to camp.
I've been trying to. Just can't stop thinking about... everything.
What would you rather think of then?
...I don't know.
There must be something. A warm fire? Your pipe? Hot food?
Mmmmmh... food...
Oh? What kind?

Wyit?

...Oh.

Pleasant dreams then.

Whatever it is you dream of.

The End

Béisbol 2

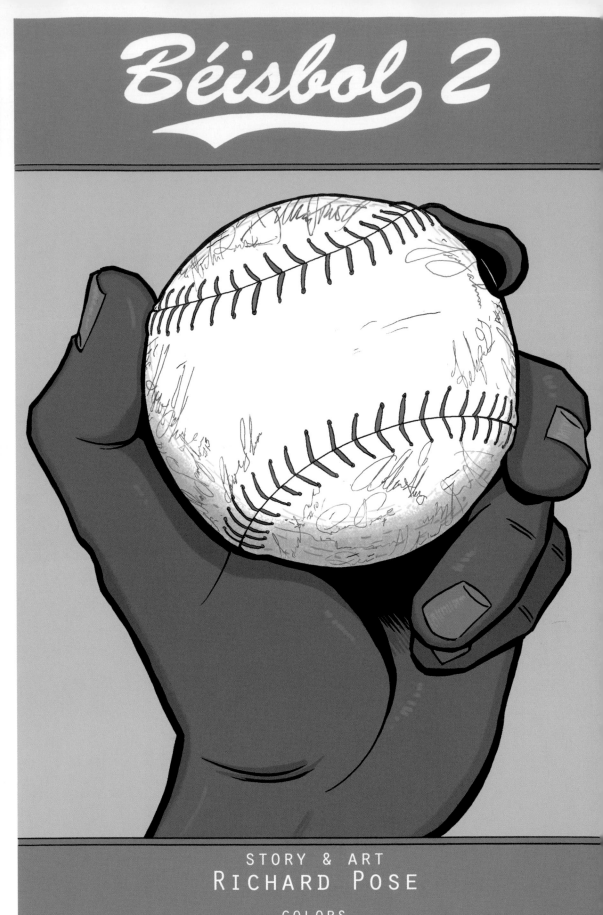

STORY & ART
RICHARD POSE

COLORS
ISRAEL SANCHEZ & MIKE ROUSH

WAIT MISTER...

I'M SAVING THE "SWEET SPOT"...

...CAN YOU SIGN HERE PLEASE?

SURE KID...
...NO PROBLEM.
WHO IS HE?
...CAN'T FIND HIS CARD...
ANY BATS OR BALLS THAT GO INTO STANDS

SO, YOU LIKE THE KINGFISH, HUH?
UH-HUH.

LOOKS LIKE YOU'VE ALMOST GOT EVERY PLAYER.
YEAH...

...EXCEPT SOME ROOKIES AND THE BOPPER...
...HE'S MY HERO!

WELL...
...GOOD LUCK WITH THAT ONE KID.
THANKS, MISTER!

EITHER OF YOU BOYS WANT AN AUTOGRAPH?
ANY BATS OR BALLS THAT GO INTO STANDS

NO.
NO THANKS.

JASON?...
...DO YOU EVEN KNOW WHO THAT GUY WAS?
DO YOU?
NO. WHO IS HE?

JEEZ!
YOU ARE SUCH A DORK!
I AM SO NOT RELATED TO YOU!
WELL... WHO IS HE?

THAT'S MR. SPLINTER!
HE'S A BENCHWARMER.
HE RIDES THE PINE.
HE WEARS OUT THE WOOD.
IN OTHER WORDS... HE'S A NOBODY!
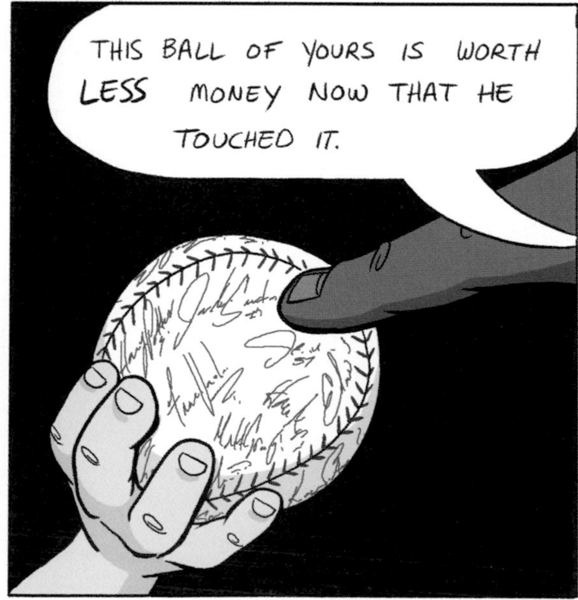
THIS BALL OF YOURS IS WORTH LESS MONEY NOW THAT HE TOUCHED IT.

I DON'T CARE WHO HE IS! HE'S A PLAYER, AND I WANT HIS AUTOGRAPH!

AND I'M NOT A DORK!...
...YOU'RE A DORK!

OH, YOU WANNA PLAY HARDBALL?
OK, THEN IF ALL YOU WANTED WAS HIS AUTOGRAPH...

THEN WHY DIDN'T YOU LET THAT "SUPERSTAR" SIGN THE SWEET SPOT?
HUH?

I JUST WANT MY HERO TO SIGN IT...
... THE BOPPER IS GOING TO SIGN IT THERE.

HA HA HA HA HA HA HA HA HA HA HA HA HA HA HA HA HA HA HA HA HA HA HA HA HA HA HA HA HA HA HA HA HA HA HA HA
PEANUTS 5.00

YOU REALLY THINK THE BOPPER'S GONNA SIGN THAT BALL FOR YOU?
MY SIDES HURT...

LISTEN, FOR STARTERS YOU AREN'T A GIRL...
...SO THAT'S STRIKE ONE!
K

AND THE GUY WON'T SIGN ANYTHING FOR FREE! LAST I HEARD, HE CHARGES $50 BUCKS...
...I KNOW YOU DON'T HAVE THAT MONEY!
SO THAT'S STRIKE TWO!
NOW SIGNING THE BOPPE
AUTOGRAPH $50
PHOTO $25
HANDSHAKE $10
EYE CONTACT $5

AND WHAT'S STRIKE THREE?

STRIKE THREE...?
...YOU'RE A SNOT... AND HE DOESN'T SIGN FOR SNOTS!!
...AND THAT'S STRIKE THREE, YOU'RE OUT!

DAIRYFARM
UTS
HE WILL TOO SIGN MY BALL!
YOU DON'T KNOW ANYTHING!

I BET HE WANTS TO GIMME HIS PHONE NUMBER SO WE CAN TALK LATER.
HI BOPPER...YEAH, I'M WATCHING... YOU TOTALLY HIT THAT HOME RUN!

AND... AND THEN, HE, MAYBE...HE WILL COME OVER AND PLAY CATCH WITH ME.

OHHHH JASON... WE CAN BE BEST FRIENDS FOREVER!
LET'S HUG NOW...

GOSH JASON!
GROW UP AND STOP BEING SO... STUPID!

I'M NOT STUPID!
YOU'RE STUPID...

MAYBE YOU SHOULD CALL HIM OVER FOR A PLAY DATE!
HE IS YOUR BEST FRIEND, RIGHT? HE IS...
22
10
1

THE BOPPER!

WHOA WHOA WHOA...
ONE QUESTION AT A TIME FOLKS!

BOPPER, HOW DO YOU FEEL NOW THAT THE TEAM IS OUT OF CONTENTION?
WELL, IT'S UNFORTUNATE.

...BUT AT LEAST NOW I WON'T HAVE THE PRESSURE OF CARRYING THIS TEAM ON MY BACK.
BOPPER
1

IT GIVES ME A CHANCE TO REALLY CONCENTRATE ON "MY" GAME...
1921
1944
MOST VALUABLE PLAYER
AMERICAN LEAGUE
THE BOPPER
CALIFORNIA KINGFISH
MEMORIAL
AWARD
...AND I'M SURE YOU'LL ALL SEE SOME VERY IMPRESSIVE NUMBERS FROM ME THIS SEASON.

BOPPER, ARE YOU GOING TO DEMAND A TRADE TO A CONTENDER?
WE HEAR THAT NEW YORK IS INTERESTED IN YOU.

OH, I WOULD **LOVE** TO PLAY IN NEW YORK!
NOW **THAT'S** A BASEBALL TOWN... BUT...

...YOU CAN'T BEAT THE SOUTHERN CALIFORNIA WEATHER...
AND ESPECIALLY THE WOMEN!

HA HA HA HA HA HA HA HAHA HA HA HA HA HA HA HA HA HA HA HA HA HA HA HA HA HA HA

EANUTS
DAIRYF
BOPPER!
BOPPER!
BOPPER!
BOPPER!
BOPPER!

BOPPER
BOPPER
BOPPER!
BOPPER
BOPPER
BOPPER

SPEAKING OF...
YOU'LL NEED TO EXCUSE ME, LADIES AND GENTS,
I NEED TO GO MEET SOME FANS.

BOPPER
1
HEY BALLBOY!
GIVE ME THAT BASEBALL YOU GOT THERE...
SANCHEZ
15
BALLBOY!

HEY KID!
YOU WANNA KEEP THIS MINIMUM WAGE GIG?!...
GIMME THAT BALL!
HEY!
SANCHEZ
15

YOU DEAF?
OR YOU JUST STUPID?
THE BOPPER JUST ASKED YOU FOR SOMETHIN'...
NOW HAND OVER THAT BALL!

I'M ES-ORRY, SEÑOR, NO KNOW YOU TALK TO ME.
I WAS JES'...
K

... EHHH...
...¿COMO SE DICE...?
...¿PRACTICA?"
...
K

¡OH, PRACTICE!
I WAS JES' PRACTICE.
K

I DON'T KNOW WHAT THE HELL YOU JUST SAID...
...AND I AM GONNA CHALK UP THE FACT THAT YOU DIDN'T GIVE ME THAT BALL TO YOU NOT SPEAKING A LICK OF ENGLISH,
BUT...

... I AIN'T ASKING AGAIN, "TONTO"...
GIVE ME THAT BALL!
??
SANC

MY NAME IS FRANCISCO, NO ES TONTO...
AND SEÑOR, I CAN NO GIVE BALL TO YOU.
I BRING THIS BALL FROM CUBA...

A GOOD FREN' GIVE TO ME...
...HE TEACH ME BÉISB–

POP
!!!
HOLY CRAP!

I DIDN'T ASK FOR YOUR LIFE STORY...
...I ASKED FOR THAT BASEBALL!

NOW YOU LISTEN TO ME...
I DON'T CARE IF YOU'RE FROM TIMBUKTU...
IS CUBA.
...BUT IF YOU KEEP THIS UP...

...I WILL DAMN WELL MAKE SURE THAT YOU'LL END UP ROTTING ON THE PINE...
...OF SOME BACKWATER MINOR LEAGUE TEAM!
BOPPER

WHO THE HELL DO YOU THINK YOU ARE ANYWAYS?
THAT BALL IS FOR A FAN! ARE YOU GOING TO LET DOWN THE FANS FOR SOME DIRTY PIECE OF HIDE?
IF I WERE YOU, I WOULD STOW THAT ATTITUDE AND START LEARNING THE LANGUAGE.
YOU ARE AT A CROSSROADS, BOY!
BOP-ME

YOU DON'T WANT TO FIND OUT WHAT I'M CAPABLE OF!...
...SO JUST HAND OVER THAT...

...
BOPPER!

BOPPER!

KEEP YER BALL...

I DON'T NEED IT ANYMORE!

WHO WANTS AN AUTOGRAPH?

HE'S COMING, JOE!
BOPPER'S COMING OVER HERE!!
LOOK!
JOE, SNAP OUT OF IT...
...GET HIS CARD READY...

THERE IS NO WAY...

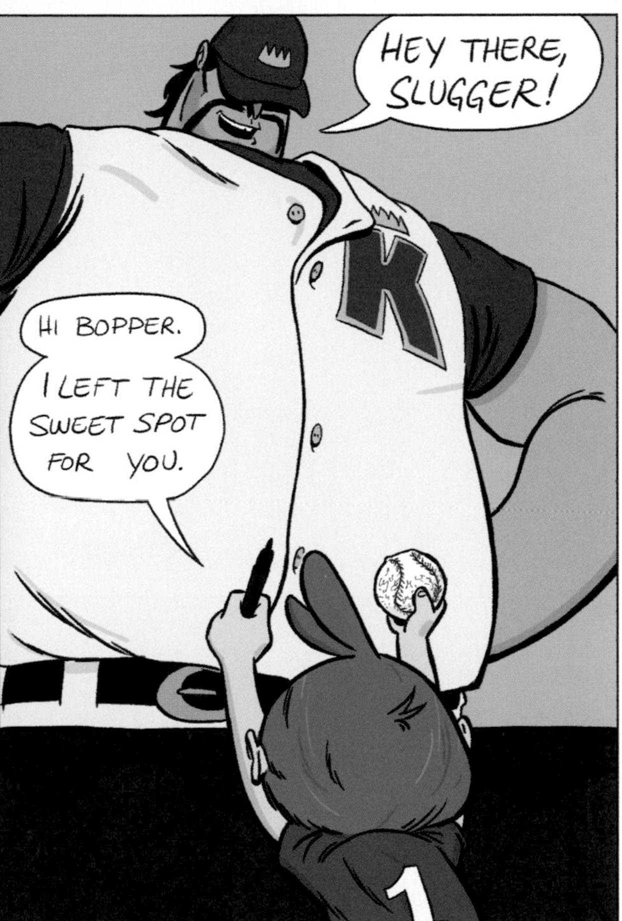
HEY THERE, SLUGGER!
HI BOPPER.
I LEFT THE SWEET SPOT FOR YOU.

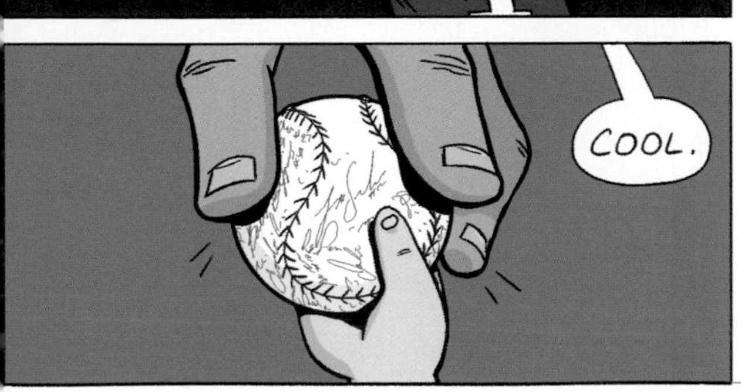
COOL.

SO...
...YOU HAVING A GOOD TIME?

YEAH, I SURE AM BOPPER...
'SPECIALLY NOW THAT YOU...

COME HERE OFTEN?

MY DAD TRIES TO BRING ME AS MUCH AS HE CAN...
...BUT HE WORKS ALOT, HE MAKES AIRPLANES.
MY MOM SOMETIMES BRINGS

SO... GIVE ME A CALL LATER, I'M SURE WE CAN THINK OF SOMETHING TO DO.

YEAH?!
WELL, MAYBE WE CAN PLAY CATCH?... OR...

I'LL CALL...

YOU JUST GOT ROCKED BY THE BOPPER, BABY!
BOPPER

BOPPER
1

OH MY GOSH!!
HE TOTALLY GAVE ME HIS NUMBER!!
THIS IS LIKE A DREAM!
...

THAT WAS TOTALLY A DREAM COME TRUE...
...HUH JASON?
HE HE HE

BOPPER!!
THAT WAS MY BALL!!
K

OH YEAH...
OPPER

THANKS KID.

HA HA HA HA HA HA HA HA HA HA HA HA HA HA HA HA

GET OUTTA MY WAY, MEAT.

BOPPER...

...THAT WAS MY BALL!!!

...I HAD THE WHOLE TEAM SIGN IT...
...I'VE HAD IT ALL YEAR...
...I SAVED THE SWEET SPOT FOR YOU...

PLEEEEEASE...
sigh.

LISTEN KID, THAT BALL WASN'T WORTH A DARN ANYWAYS...
...AT LEAST NOW YOU CAN TELL YOUR FRIENDS...

... YOU MET THE BOPPER!

PLUS, IF YOU KEPT THAT BALL, IT WOULDA COST YOU $50!

MA'AM,
CAN I HAVE MY BALL?
PLEASE?

HEHE
NO WAY!
THIS ONE IS ALL MINE...
...GO GET YOUR OWN BALL.

NO, WAIT!
PLEASE!
HA

SANCHEZ
15
PLEASE...
HA HA HA

HA HA HA HA HA HA HA HA HA HA HA HA HA HA HA HA HA HA HA HA HA HA HA HA HA HA HA HA HA
SNIFF
SNIFF
SNIFF

HA HA HA HA HA HA HA HA HA HA HA HA HA
SOB

OYE NIÑO
NO LLORES
SOB
NO CRY, ¿OK?

SNNNIFFF

¿YOU SEE?

K
SNIFF

NO CRY...
THAT'S BETTER,
¿NO?

NO.
SANCHEZ
15

¿NO?...
¿WHAT HAPPEN TO YOU?

THE BOPPER TOOK MY BASEBALL...
OK.
...AND...

...HE SIGNED IT AND HE WAS LIKE MY FAVORITE PLAYER AND I WAS HAPPY AND THEN HE WAS TALKING TO ME AND THEN HE WANTED TO HANG OUT BUT THEN HE GAVE MY BALL TO A GIRL! YUCK!, AND I HAVE HAD THAT BALL THIS WHOLE SEASON AND I HAVE EVERYONE'S AUTOGRAPH AND NOW THAT GIRL HAS IT AND THEN THE BOPPER WAS LIKE...

HAHAHA...
...OK OK...
...I SEE...

... HE WAS MY HERO...

I HATE HIM...
SOB
I HATE HIM...
...I HATE HIM...

AND...
I HATE BASEBALL!

OK, OK,
NO LLORES.

LOOK...
THIS IS A BASEBALL I BRING FROM CUBA.
CUBA WAS MY HOME.
WHAT'S THAT?

MY NEIGHBOR THERE, SEÑOR GONZALEZ, HE GIVE ME THIS BALL. HE WAS LIKE GRANDFATHER TO ME...
FRANCISCO, ACUERDATE, NUNCA QUITES LA VISTA DE LA PELOTA.
¡NUNCA!
... HE WAS VERY HELPFUL, HE TEACH ME HOW TO PLAY BEÍSBOL...

... AND HE TEACH ME THAT DREAMS CAN BE REACHED...
ADIOS, SEÑOR,
ADIOS, MAMÁ, PAPÁ...
... ADIOS, CUBA LINDA...
... BUT SOMETIMES TO GET A DREAM, IT CAN HURT VERY MUCH.

THIS IS ALL I HAVE LEFT...
THIS BALL VERY SPECIAL TO ME...

... BUT...
...IF YOU WANT, I GIVE YOU THIS BASEBALL...
BUT I NO GIVE FOR FREE...
WE MAKE A DEAL.

THE DEAL IS THAT I GIVE YOU BALL IF YOU EH-STOP CRYING...
...AND I WAN' YOU TO WATCH ONE MORE GAME...
...DON'T GIVE UP ON BEÍSBOL YET. IT'S A GOOD GAME.

¿DEAL?

SNIFF

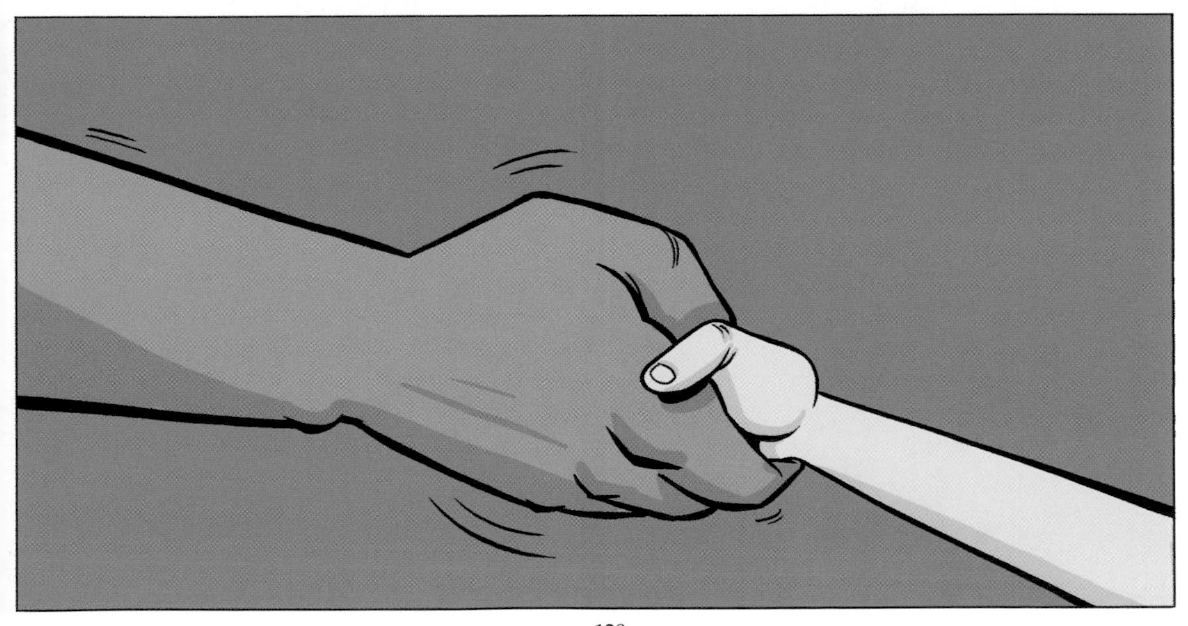

OHHHH...
¡MUY FUERTE!
¡VERY EH-STRONG!

YOU ARE GOING TO BE O.K.

HERE YOU GO, NIÑO.

TAKE CARE OF THAT BALL...
...PLEASE.
SANCHEZ
15

HEY, MISTER?

¿EH?
CAN YOU SIGN THE BALL?
¡HA HA! ¿COMO NO?

JASON!
WHAT ARE YOU DOING?
THAT GUY IS AN UBER-NO NAME!

HAVE FUN TODAY... ¿OK?
HEHE OK.

DORK.

FIND YOUR SEATS BOYS. THE GAME IS ABOUT TO START.
YES SIR.

BOPPER
1

WHAT THE...!
BOPPER
1

HANDS OFF!!

¡¿WHAT IS WRONG WITH YOU?! YOU STOLE THAT BOY'S BALL !¿WHAT KIND OF MAN WOULD STEAL FROM A CHILD? WELL, I CAN TELL YOU THAT...
?

¡... LOS NINÕS NO SE PUEDEN TRATAR ASI! ¿ME ESTAS ASIENDO CASO? ¡¿EH?! ESE NIÑO ESTABA LLORANDO...¿ESO NO TE IMPORTA? TU NI SABES LO QUE TU ERES...
SANCH

¡...YOU ARE A HERO TO THESE KIDS, AND YOU, YOU JUST STEAL THEIR DREAMS!
YOU ARE NO HERO, SEÑOR BOPPER.
¡YOU ARE A SMALL MAN!

I DON'T SPEAK MEXICAN...
... BUT I GOT THE GIST!
YOU THINK YOU'RE HOT STUFF, HUH?
YOU BEST LISTEN UP, BOY...

I AM THE HEART AND SOUL OF THIS TEAM! AND YOU?
YOU AIN'T **NOTHIN'!** JUST SOME DUMB ROOKIE...
... SO I AM GOING TO CUT YOU SOME SLACK...

... YOU JUST BETTER GET OUTTA MY FACE BEFORE THINGS GET NASTY.

HE HE

OHHH......
HELL NO...

NO NO...
...THE BOPPER IS GREAT. HE'S NOT A DISTRACTION AT ALL...
SKIP?
YEAH?

I THINK YOU HAVE A PROBLEM, SKIP.
AH CRUD.
EXCUSE ME.

WHAT I TELL YA?

WHOA! WHOA!
DAMN IT BOPPER...
WHAT THE DEMON IS GOING ON HERE!

YOU!
GET BACK TO STRETCHIN' OR I SWEAR...
SI SEÑOR.

...AND YOU BOPPER!! I AM STILL YOUR MANAGER AND IF YOU DON'T START PARTICIPATING IN THIS "TEAM" SPORT...
... I'LL BENCH YA!!

YOU AIN'T GOT THE GUTS, SKIP...
AND IT DON'T MATTER 'CAUSE AFTER THIS SEASON, YOU'LL BE GONE...
...AND I'LL STILL REIGN OVER THIS TEAM.
SKIPPER
0

#@!%

JUST DO SOMETHING!
...ANYTHING!

YEAH, WHATEVER YOU WANT, "SKIP."
AND I'LL SEE YOU LATER, LOSER!

SANC

WHAT YOU WAITING FOR? GET MOVIN'!
WE'VE GOT A GAME TO PLAY!

I HATE THIS JOB...

WELCOME TO ANOTHER EXCITING CALIFORNIA KINGFISH BALL GAME!
IT PROMISES TO BE A BEAUTIFUL DAY FOR BASEBALL...
... AND IT LOOKS LIKE BOTH TEAMS ARE JUST ABOUT READY TO GET THIS GAME UNDER WAY.

THE PITCHER IS FINISHING UP HIS WARM-UP TOSSES...

...THE PLAYERS ARE TAKING THE FIELD...
LISTEN TO THOSE CHEERS, I GUESS IT'S EASY TO SEE WHO THE HOMETOWN HERO IS.

THE FANS ARE STILL FILING INTO THEIR SEATS.
LOOKS LIKE WE'RE JUST ABOUT READY TO GET UNDER WAY... SO LET'S...

...PLAY BALL!!

THERE HE IS, JASON...
...YOU WERE RIGHT TO GET HIS AUTOGRAPH...

...IT'LL BE WORTH MILLIONS!!!
YOU THINK?
OH MY GOSH, YOU ARE A WEINER!
HEY, THE BOPPER IS UP.
YOU ARE.

HEY JASON, YOUR HERO IS UP TO BAT. YOU GONNA CRY?
BETCHA HE WALLOPS ONE!
NOPE, I MADE A DEAL.
UHHH... DORK!

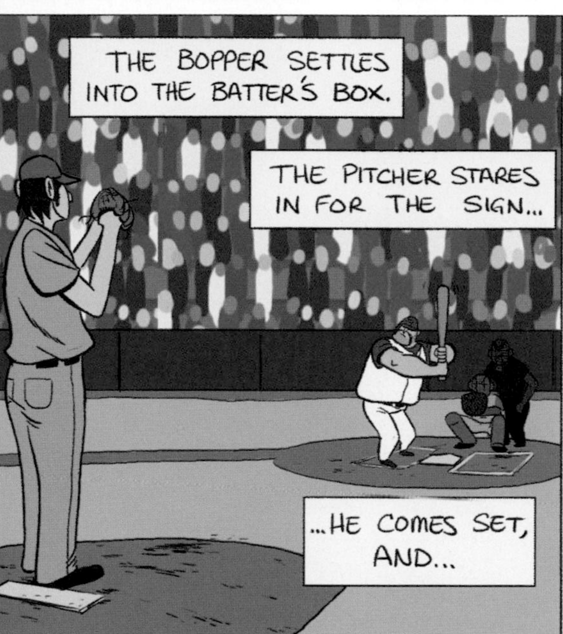
THE BOPPER SETTLES INTO THE BATTER'S BOX.
THE PITCHER STARES IN FOR THE SIGN...
...HE COMES SET, AND...

...HERE'S THE PITCH...
WHOA!! THIS ONE IS HIGH AND DEEP!!
THIS IS WHAT THE FANS LOVE TO SEE!

IF IT STAYS FAIR...
...IT IS WAAAY OUTTA HERE...

...OHHHH, IT JUST SLICES FOUL!
WELL, THE BOPPER JUST WHET OUR APPETITE, LET'S SEE IF HE DELIVERS THE MAIN COURSE!

	1	2	3	4	5	6	7	8	9	10	RUNS	HITS	ERR
SLIMEBALLS	0										0	0	0
KINGFISH	0										0	0	0

AT BAT 38 BALL 0 STRIKE 0 OUT 0

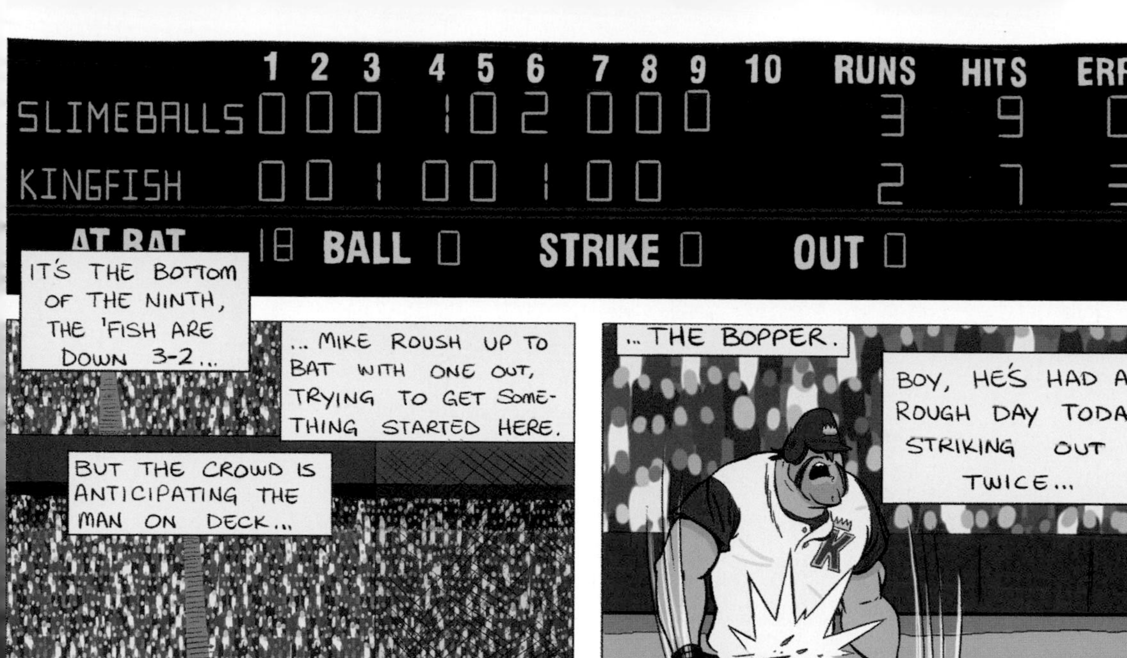

1 2 3 4 5 6 7 8 9 10 RUNS HITS ERR
SLIMEBALLS 0 0 0 1 0 2 0 0 0 3 9 0
KINGFISH 0 0 1 0 0 1 0 0 2 7 3
AT BAT 18 BALL 0 STRIKE 0 OUT 0
IT'S THE BOTTOM OF THE NINTH, THE 'FISH ARE DOWN 3-2...

... MIKE ROUSH UP TO BAT WITH ONE OUT, TRYING TO GET SOMETHING STARTED HERE.
BUT THE CROWD IS ANTICIPATING THE MAN ON DECK...

... THE BOPPER.
BOY, HE'S HAD A ROUGH DAY TODAY, STRIKING OUT TWICE...
AND I GET THE FEELING HE DIDN'T LIKE THE CALLS

HE'S ALSO GROUNDED INTO A DOUBLE PLAY...
...AND COMMITED TWO ERRORS IN THE FIELD.
OOPS.
CRAP!
HURRY UP... THEY'RE SCORING
HUFF HUFF
...ONE OF WHICH LED TO TWO UNEARNED RUNS.

LOOKING DOWN TO THE ON-DECK CIRCLE, ONE WONDERS
WHERE IS THE BOPPER?

WHAT THE...?
BOPPER!!

IT'S COOL, BABE, GAME'LL BE OVER IN A SEC, THEN...
BOPPER!

...WE CAN MEET BACK AT MY PLACE...
YER ON DECK!!
K
SKIP
0

GET OFF THE DAG GUM PHONE AND GET ON DECK!

WOW
CHILL OUT, OLD-TIMER.
...

SO IF YOUR FRIEND WANTS TO COME...
WHAT DID YOU SAY!!
HOLD ON,
LISTEN, SKIP, THIS GAME IS ALMOST OVER...

BUT IT ISN'T!!
AND YOU'VE BEEN PLAYIN' ALL DAY AS IF YOU'VE GOT SOMEPLACE YOU'D RATHER BE.

CRACK
...AND ROUSH PULLS INTO SECOND BASE WITH A DOUBLE INTO RIGHT FIELD.
WITH ONE OUT AND A MAN ON SECOND, A BASE HIT CAN TIE IT!

LISTEN TO THIS CROWD...
HEY BABE, I GOTTA GO DO MY THING.
THEY KNOW WHO'S UP TO BAT, AND THEY EXPECT THIS GAME TO END WITH ONE SWING.

SEE YOU IN AN HOUR, BYE.

DUDE, SEASON'S DONE! THIS CRAP OF A TEAM IS IN LAST PLACE...
I'LL GO DO MY THING, MAKE THE FANS CHEER,
AND THEN I CAN GO HOME AND HAVE REAL FUN...

...AND GET THE HELL AWAY FROM YOU AND ALL THESE OTHER LOSERS!

KID!
BOPPER 1

GRAB A BAT!

YOU SPEAK ENGLISH?
JES.

WELL THEN! GRAB A BAT!!
SI SEÑOR

WHAT THE...!?

SKIP!
WHAT THE HELL YA PLAYIN' AT?
I'M BENCHIN' YA, BOPPER.

WHAT!

YOU'RE BENCHIN' THE BEST BAT IN BASEBALL WITH A CRAP ROOKIE!!
YOU'RE REPLACIN' ME WITH SOME TWO-CENT HACK NO NAME?!

I CAN WIN THIS GAME, RIGHT NOW.
ONE SWING!
I WILL HIT IT OUT!

GO HIT THE SHOWERS...
...YOUR SEASON IS OVER...
...GO HAVE SOME "FUN."

YOU BETTER ENJOY THIS AT-BAT...
...IT'S GONNA BE YOUR LAST!
I AM A FIXTURE HERE...
...YOU'RE A NOBODY!!

LOOKS LIKE WE'RE GOING TO HAVE A PINCH HITTER HERE...
HOLA SEÑOR UMPIRE.
SHOVE IT!

I'M ASSUMING THE BOPPER IS INJURED; OTHERWISE, THIS JUST IS NOT A SMART MOVE.
THE UNKNOWN BATTER IS DIGGING IN...

...AND AS SOON AS I GET SOME INFORMATION ON THIS PLAYER, I WILL PASS IT ALONG.
NO WAY!!

BOOOO
BOOOOO
BOOOOO
BOOOO
BOOOOOOOOO

THE "BOO BIRDS" ARE OUT IN FORCE TODAY.

THE KID SETTLES INTO THE BATTER'S BOX...
...THE PITCHER FINDS THE SIGN HE LIKES...

HERE'S THE WIND UP...
... AND THE PITCH.

STREEE-RIKE
WHIFFFFF
THE BATTER WAS BADLY FOOLED ON THAT BREAKING BALL.

EH-TIME OUT.
TIME!
TIME IS CALLED, AND LISTEN TO THESE FANS LAYING IT ON!

THE KID STEPS BACK INTO THE BOX.
COUNT IS NO BALLS, ONE STRIKE.

PITCHER LOOKS IN FOR THE SIGN.
HE'S GOT THE ONE HE WANTS
HERE'S THE 0-1 PITCH...

CURVE...

POW

THE KID LINES A BASE HIT TO CENTER...
...THAT'S GOING TO DRIVE IN THE TYING RUN!
KINGFISH

HE'S NOT STOPPING AT FIRST!!

HE'S GOING FOR TWO!!
TWO! TWO!
AH CRUD.

HERE'S THE THROW!
UHHH!

SAFE!!
SAFE ON A CLOSE PLAY!

THIS KID HAS, AT LEAST, QUIETED THE FANS FOR THE TIME BEING.
BOPPER WOULDA HIT IT OUT...
REALLY WALLOPED IT
I DON'T KNOW...
SMOKED...
HE LACED IT.
FROZEN ROPE
I WANTED THE BOPPER...
HE GOT LUCKY.
YOU STILL SUCK!
WE DON'T HAVE HIS NAME YET, BUT HE SPORTS THE NUMBER 15, AND HE'S GOT WHEELS!

THE 'FISH NOW HAVE THE WINNING RUN IN SCORING POSITION WITH LESS THAN TWO OUTS...
...A BASE HIT CAN WIN THE GAME!
SANCHEZ
15
THE KID TAKES HIS LEAD...

THE BALL SKIPS AWAY FROM THE CATCHER...
... BUT NOT FAR ENOUGH FOR THE RUNNER TO...

WHOA!
THREE!
THE KID IS HEADED TO THIRD!!

THE CATCHER RECOVERS QUICKLY...
...THIS IS GOING TO BE ANOTHER CLOSE PLAY!!

IS HE...?
SAFE!
WHOA NELLY!

THIS KID SURE IS ELECTRIFYING THE BASEPATHS
WOW!
WIPE WIPE
WHO IS HE?

EXCITING
NAME?
HE'S NOT IN THE PROGRAM
FAST
WHO IS THAT?
BOPPER CAN'T DO THAT...
WHOA
HE'S JUST GOT "ROOKIE LUCK"!
DUDE, HE'S FAST.
WHO?
WHAT'S HIS NAME?
FASTER THAN GREASED LIGHTNING
I NEED TO BUY HIS JERSEY...

THE KID TAKES A LEAD AS THE HITTER STEPS IN...
PITCHER LOOKS OVER AT THIRD...

PICK-OFF PLAY AT THIRD!
BACK

SAFE
TOO CLOSE

WHAT IS THIS KID DOING?
A SACRIFICE FLY COULD WIN THE GAME.
LAST THING WE NEED IS A PICK OFF

THE PITCHER STARES HIM DOWN...
...HE TURNS HOME, HERE'S THE...

THE KID IS OFF!!

THERE'S GONNA BE A PLAY AT THE PLATE!
THIS COULD COST THE 'FISH THE WIN!

IS HE SAFE?
OUT?
SANCHEZ
15

SAFE!

¿QUIETO?

PRUETT
17
SPANGLER
7
RID
8
ROUSH

¡AYE CARAMBA!
WHOA!
WAY TO RUN
ALRIGHT!
..KID!
GO
NICE
YES

GET ME THAT KID'S NAME!!
YOU GOT IT SKIP.

WE SHOULD HAVE GOTTEN HIS AUTOGRAPH, HUH?

JASON, I'LL GIVE YOU $5 FOR THE BALL...
WONDER IF I HAVE HIS CARD...
...JASON...?
...JASON...?
DO YOU KNOW HIS NAME?

JASON, $10... FINAL OFFER!
JASON?... JASON? WHO WAS THAT GUY?
YOU KNOW WHO THAT WAS?
NO, BUT I KNOW WHAT THIS IS...
...HIGH FIVE!!
KF: 4
SB: 3
PEANUTS
THAT GUY WAS GREAT!
WHO IS HE?!

DOES ANYONE KNOW WHO THAT GUY IS?!

Francisco Sanchez

HE'S MY HERO.

THE COURIER

by Kazu Kibuishi

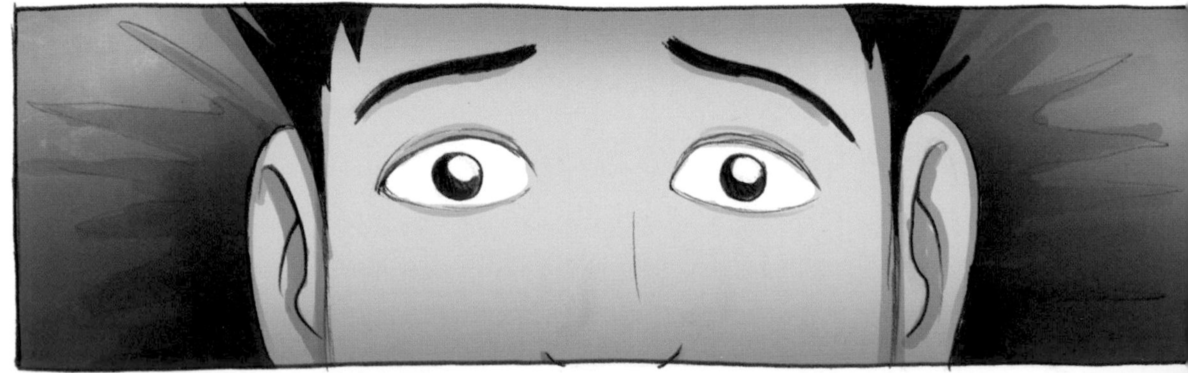

WHAT DO YOU MEAN YOU DON'T KNOW?!
HOW COULD I HAVE KNOWN?!
I HEAR A LOT OF THINGS THROUGH THESE WALLS.

MY NEIGHBORS SAY THEY HATE WHAT THE WORLD HAS BECOME, BUT I THINK THEY'RE JUST VENTING THEIR FRUSTRATIONS FROM BEING IN A BAD MARRIAGE.
JUST SHUT UP!!

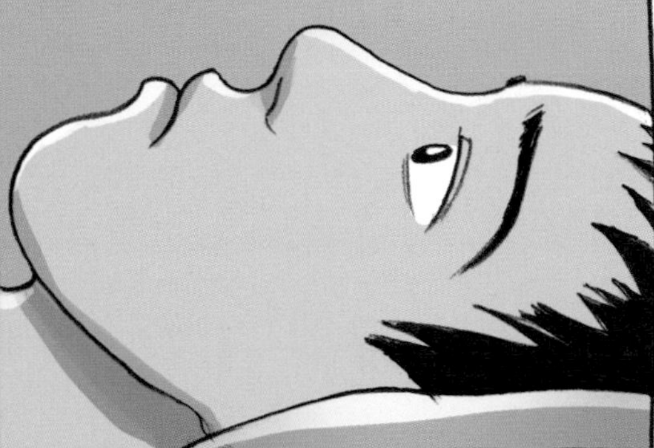
BAM!
GOOD, CLEAR COMMUNICATION IS IMPORTANT, SO WHY DOES IT HAVE TO SEEM LIKE A RARE COMMODITY?

BEEP! BEEP! BEEP!
KDUNK!

THIS ONE'S HIGH PRIORITY, SO NO MESSIN' AROUND, KID!

OH GOOD. FAMILIAR TERRITORY.
TO: 701 MARSH ST
URGENT
I'LL TAKE THE SCENIC ROUTE.

MY JOB IS TO CARRY INFORMATION ACROSS THE GRID. THEY NEVER TELL ME WHAT IT'S ABOUT, AND I'M NOT SUPPOSED TO ASK.
NOT KNOWING CAN BE PRETTY FRUSTRATING AT TIMES.

FFT!
THIS IS IT.

MY LAST RUN.
SHK!

I FIXED THE WASHER YESTERDAY, MISS WILSON.
THANK YOU SO MUCH, TOM.
BE CAREFUL ON YOUR DELIVERY.
I'VE TAKEN A NUMBER OF ODD JOBS SINCE COMING TO THE CITY,
BUT BEING A COURIER IS THE FIRST ONE I STUCK WITH.

IT'S A PRETTY THANKLESS JOB.

BUT I KEEP DOING RUNS...

SO I CAN PAY THE BILLS.

AND THAT SHOULDN'T BE WHY I DO THIS. I SHOULD BE WORKING FOR SOMETHING BEYOND MY SURVIVAL.
I NEED TO HAVE A PURPOSE.

THAT'S WHY I NEED TO LEAVE...
THE WHOLE WORLD IS WAITING FOR ME OUT THERE.

OKAY, TIME TO FOCUS.
KEEP MY HEAD CLEAR...
BIG BIG
HAVE NO FEAR.

MOVE LIKE WATER.

AND FIND THE FASTEST AND MOST DIRECT ROUTE...

EVEN IF IT MEANS CAUSING SOME TROUBLE.

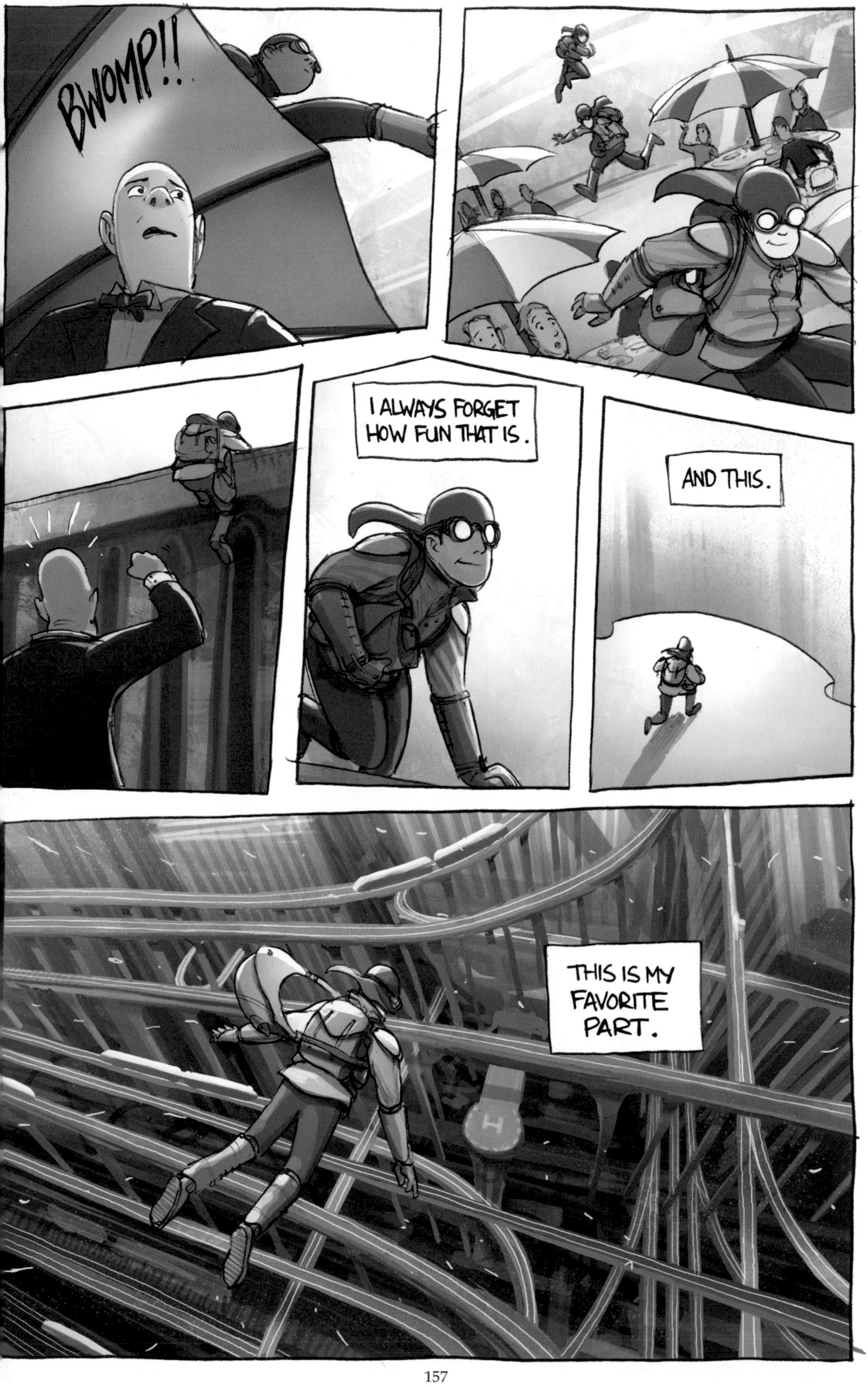

BWOMP!!

I ALWAYS FORGET HOW FUN THAT IS.

AND THIS.

THIS IS MY FAVORITE PART.

FWOOOMP!

MY LAST MISSION.
I BETTER LAND THIS RIGHT.

BEEP!
BEEP!
BEEP!
KDUNK!
I THINK I'LL STICK TO THIS JOB FOR NOW.

I MUST BE DOING SOMETHING RIGHT.

Malinky Robot

MALINKY ROBOT

"Karakuri"

$1.99 Sonny Liew

red robot

THIS IS
HEAVY STUFF!
HEAVY
HEAVY
YEAH YOU
BETTER BE
TREATING US TO
SOME *GOOD* FOOD
MR. NABISCO!

HEH ASSUREDLY,
ASSUREDLY...

WHERE'D YOU GET
THE *MONEY* TO MOVE
OUT HERE ANYWAY?

HMMM...
LET'S JUST SAY
A FEW INVESTMENTS
CAME GOOD...
HNUH...

JUST PUT THEM IN THE CORNER NEAR THE SHELVES.
UH!

THAT'S *HEAVY*! HEY MISTER NABISCO YOU GOT ANY WA–

HELLO

HEY!
IT'S A... IT'S A...

I AM A ROBOT
IT'S A ROBOT!
HAVEN'T SEEN ONE LIKE THIS BEFORE...

...AND MOST OF ALL, SIMULATING THE SOUNDS OF RAINSWEPT DAYS ON TIN ROOF AWNINGS IN THE NIGHT TIME...

REAL ROBOTS SHOOT LASERS FROM HIDDEN COMPARTMENTS!

SOME HAVE THE ABILITY TO TRANSFORM FROM ORDINARY OBJECTS...

THERE ARE MANY YOU CAN TAKE A RIDE IN...

THEY SMASH THINGS!!

...SOME OF THEM PROTECT THE WEAK AND INNOCENT...

CHECKMATE IN SEVENTY-FOUR!
WHILST OTHERS HAVE INCREDIBLE MATHEMATICS ABILITIES...

...AND MOST OF ALL...
THEY FIGHT OTHER ROBOTS WHILST FLYING HIGH ABOVE THE CITY!!

SO...THIS FELLOW...
MMM... MORE AN APPLIANCE!
HEY!
HEH... PERHAPS PERHAPS...
PEKING DUCK AT THE SOUP KING?
YES!
REMEMBER TO RECORD SUPER GIANT Z AT EIGHT!
这一切是通过一个内置摄像头发射的视频和音频实现的，使用者通过此途径监测机器人反应的周边情况

通过输送实时视频和
音频，让使用者即使远在
天边，也可以
用，效果得到了业
肯定。"北极星
航系统扮演了微型
I AM
A ROBOT

WORRY DOLLS
Story and art JP AHONEN
Colors MARJAANA MALKAMÄKI
JP AHONEN

SNIFT
NOTICE

KLAK

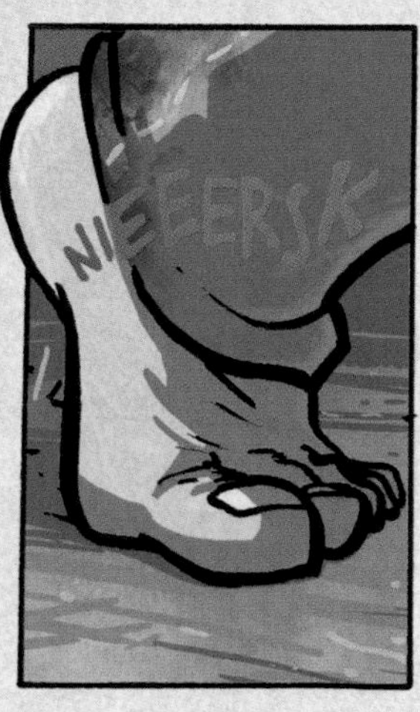
NIEEERSK

TI DI DI DI
TA DA TA DI
TII

TA DA DA
TII DI DA DI
DI DAA
HAH! YOU TRYING TO SNEAK PAST ME, MR. MOORE?

TA DA DA
DA DII
DI DI
WOULDN'T DREAM OF IT!
I'M ORGANIZING IT.
SO WHERE'S MY RENT?
WHAT'S THERE TO ORGANIZE? YOU. MONEY. GIVE. SIMPLE AS THAT!
TOMORROW, OKAY? NOW I SHOULD REALLY—
WELL YOU BETTER HAVE IT BY TOMORROW OR I'LL KICK YOU OUT! AND WHAT IS THAT GOD FORSAKEN RACKET?! TURN IT OFF!
WELL I WAS GOING TO.

IF YOU D— WAIT A MINUTE!
GOTTA RUN, SORRY! I'LL HAVE THE MONEY TOMORROW.
WELL YOU-
TI DI DII DA DA TA DAA

TI DI DA DI DA TI
SLAM!

Selma is calling...
DA TA DA DII

HON, I'M HOME!
HONEY?
AWW CRAP.
TI DI DI DA DA

HEY... WHERE ARE Y... NO, I DIDN'T FORGET, I JUST, I WAS AT THE AUDITION AND... NAH, DIDN'T GET IT.
APPARENTLY I DON'T HAVE THE RIGHT FACE.

WELL I DON'T KNOW, A FACE THAT'D ETCH ITSELF INTO PEOPLE MINDS? ASK THE DIRECTOR OR SOMETHING.
BUT HEY, I WANTED TO TELL YOU...
FOR MATT

...THAT I'M SORRY. IT'S JUST...
YOU...YOU ALWAYS PULL IT TOGETHER AND...
SUCCEED IN EVERYTHING. YOU'RE DOING YOUR THING AND I'M...
WELL I'M JUST A STRUGGLING ACTOR WITHOUT A JOB, MONEY TO PAY THE RENT AND...
WHO'S...
WHO'S AFRAID OF LOSING YOU.
MUSCL
Sleep
NIVE
AND FRANKLY FORGETTING OUR ANNIVERSARY ISN'T IMPROVING THINGS EITHER...
I'M SORRY.
I REALLY AM...
BUT I'LL MAKE IT UP TO—
OKAY. I UNDERSTAND. SAY HI TO YOUR PARENTS. TALK TO YOU LATER THEN.

Happy anniversary my love! I know you've been under a lot of stress lately so that's why the absurd gift.
Genuine Guatemalan worry dolls. Hope they'll get your mind off things.
XXX Selma

OH SELMA ...

AND I COULDN'T EVEN AFFORD TO GET YOU ANYTHING...
SOMETHING TROUBLING
NOT TO WORRY! SHARE
TROUBLES WITH THE
PLACE THEN UNDERNEATH
THE WORRIES DISAPPEAR

OKAY...

WHAT STRESSES ME OUT IS... NOT HAVING WORK.
AND THEREFORE NOT HAVING MONEY TO PAY THE BILLS.
AND... BEING SO PATHETIC SELMA WILL LEAVE ME...
I MEAN, LOOK. I'M TALKING TO COTTON DOLLS NOW.

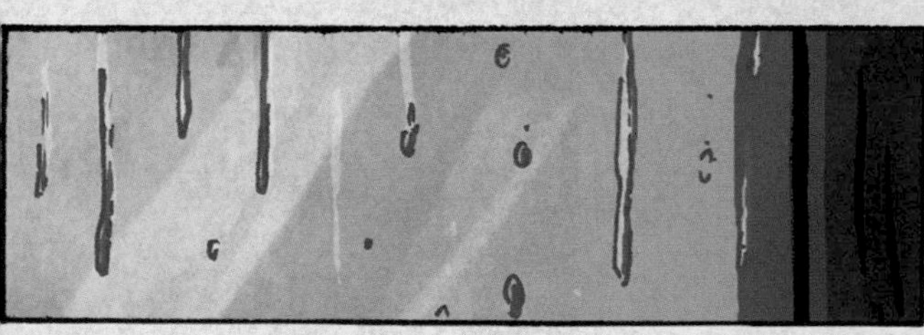

so that's why the
absurd gift! —
genuine Guatemalan
worry dolls. Hope
'll get your

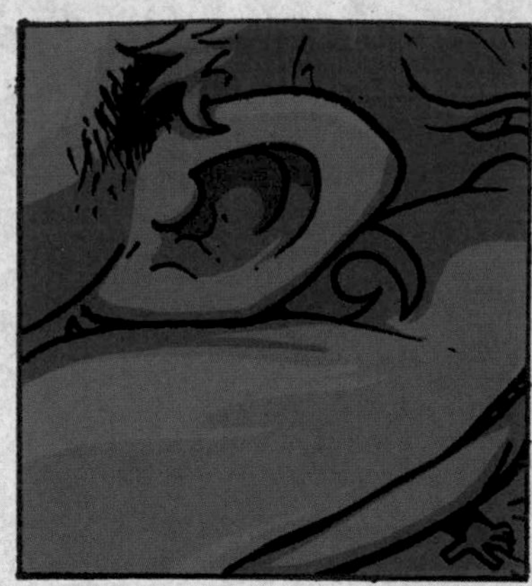

HNNGH!

OKAYYY... TIME TO GET TO WORK.
LEAD THE WAY, CARLOS.
WHOA! LOOK AT THE SIZE OF THAT THING! I THINK THIS IS THE CLOSEST I'VE EVER BEEN TO AN ACTUAL HUMAN!

WELL, THESE DON'T ACTUALLY DIFFER THAT MUCH FROM THE DUMMIES USED IN TRAINING.
BUT DUMMIES DON'T WAKE UP, WHAT IF THIS ONE DOES?

WHAT? AFRAID HE'LL WAKE UP, ROBERTO?
STOP IT, CARLOS.

COME ON, GABRIELLE.
FLAPTH

NOW ONCE WE'RE IN THERE, DON'T TOUCH ANYTHING UNLESS I SAY SO, GOT IT, ROBERTO?
YES, M'AM.

LOOK AT ALL THESE IMAGES!

THIS FELLOW IS ONE TWISTED—

OH BOY, THIS IS CRAMMED.

CARLOS! AS YOU WELL KNOW, WE PREFER THE WORD "CLIENT."
NOW...

WHAT WE DO HERE, ROBERTO, IS A SORT OF CLEANSING. TOUCH THE IMAGE SOFTLY, SCALE IT SMALLER, AND CHUCK IT OUT.

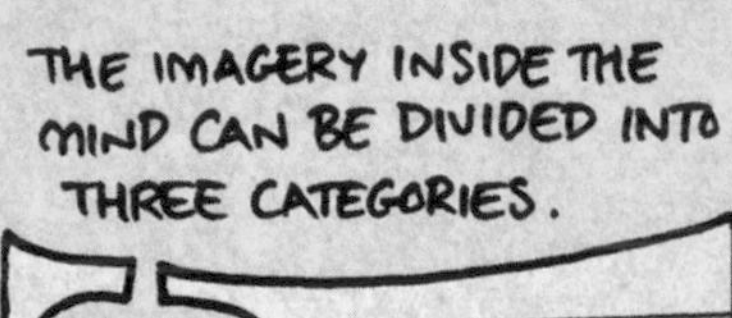
THE IMAGERY INSIDE THE MIND CAN BE DIVIDED INTO THREE CATEGORIES.

HOPES.
007
ANTUM
SOLACE

FEARS.

AND MEMORIES. WE SHOULD ALWAYS LEAVE A FEW WARM ONES INSIDE.

ANY QUESTIONS? THINK YOU'LL MANAGE?
YUP. ALL'S GOOD

SO WHERE DO THE IMAGES GO EXACTLY, AFTER GETTING THROWN OUT?
THEY END UP IN THE EXTERNAL AUDITORY CANAL.

THE CLIENTS CALL IT "EAR WAX," WE PREFER "PROCESSED DATA."

WOW! I WOULD'VE NEVER THOUGHT IT'D BE THIS HIGH TECH.
WELL EVERYTHING CHANGED AFTER WE WENT PUBLIC WITH OUR STOCK.

YIKES!
BYEW!
WHAT'S THAT?

I—I—I DON'T KNOW, THERE WAS A BLACK IMAGE AT FIRST BUT—BUT...
...THEN THE IMAGE CHANGED INTO THIS BLURRY THING! BUT I SWEAR I DID EVERYTHING AS INSTRUCTED!

WHAT IS THAT?
THE IMAGE IS SHARPENING.
THAT LOOKS SLIGHTLY FAMILIAR ...

OH DEAR!
WHAT? WHAT IS IS IT? AM I FIRED?
AM I FIRED NOW?!
I'M AFRAID WHAT WE'RE SEEING HERE IS NEITHER A HOPE, NOR A FEAR, NOR A MEMORY.

IT'S THE PRESENT.

BUT NOT TO WORRY. THE CLIENT RESPONDS TO IMPULSES, SO BY PRESSING THE CORRECT NEURON, WE'LL GET HIM BACK TO LULLABYLAND.

TZHK

RASHAAANGH

OW!
UGH!
BUNT

WELL THAT WENT WELL.

BUT I DON'T UNDERSTAND! THIS IS THE RIGHT SPOT, HOW COME IT RESPONDED LIKE THIS?
KEEP YOUR HANDS OFF! FOR SOME REASON THE CLIENT IS MALFUNCTIONING. COULD BE UNDER SOME SORT OF DRUG OR EVEN MENTALLY ILL... THAT'D EXPLAIN WHY THE PRESENT STATE IMAGE SHOWED UP HERE IN THE FIRST PLACE.

OUR CLIENT ISN'T EXACTLY AWAKE NOR ASLEEP. HE MUST BE SEDATED SOMEHOW, OTHERWISE HE WOULD HAVE WOKEN UP ALREADY.
SO WE'LL HAVE TO BAIL OUT?
NEVERTHELESS WE MUST BE CAREFUL. IF HE WAKES UP WITH US INSIDE, HE'LL BASICALLY GO INSANE. OUR PERSON-ALITIES WOULD MERGE WITH HIS, CAUSING SCHIZOPHRENIA.

AND LEAVE THE CLIENT LIKE THIS? YOU WANT TO LOSE YOUR JOB, CARLOS? WANT TO GO BACK TO BEING A RAGDOLL?
WELL, NOT REALLY.

SO OUR ONLY CHANCE IS TO GET THIS MAN UP, BACK TO BED, AND ASLEEP.

AFRAID SO. CONCENTRATE. TRY TO FIND THE RIGHT NEURONS.
KZZT

THAT'S IT! THAT'S THE WAY TO GO!

YES! AND A BIT TOO FAST, IF I MAY ADD! B-BUT DON'T STOP!

WHY NOT?

HOOONKK

WE'RE IN THE MIDDLE OF TRAFFIC!

HEY!

JERK!

SSCREECH

GOOD EVENING, SIR. SHOULDN'T YOU BE IN BED BY NOW?

umm
...

SIR, DID YOU HEAR ME?

HOW DO WE MAKE HIM TALK?
HOW THE HELL SHOULD I KNOW!?
THEY DON'T EXACTLY TEACH THIS STUFF IN TRAINING!

SIR, I'D LIKE YOU TO RAISE YOUR HANDS UP VEEERY SLOWLY.

HE'S GOING FOR THE GUN! IMPROVIZE!
!

OWW!
SORRY!
SLAPP
WHAT ARE YOU DOING, CARLOS?!
IT'S WORKING, ROBERTO! PLAY ALONG!
TAKE IT EASY NOW. COULD YOU REPEAT, PLEASE?
ERHM... SO-SORRY, OFFICER. DIDN'T MEAN ANY HARM. JUST HAVING A NICE EVENING STROLL.
OK, THAT'S ALRIGHT, BUDDY, WHAT I'D NEED YOU TO DO NOW IS RAISE YOUR HANDS.
ALRIGHTY. LET'S SEE.
NOPE. NOT THAT ONE.
NO. IT'S JUST NOT WORKING... I MUST-
APOLOGIES, OFFICER. I'M HAVING SOME PROBLEMS.

HEY! GET BACK HERE!
I DON'T KNOW HOW!

EVERYBODY DOWN!
LAST WARNING: STOP, OR I'LL SHOOT!
CAN I TAKE MY FACE OFF THE WALL NOW, CARLOS?

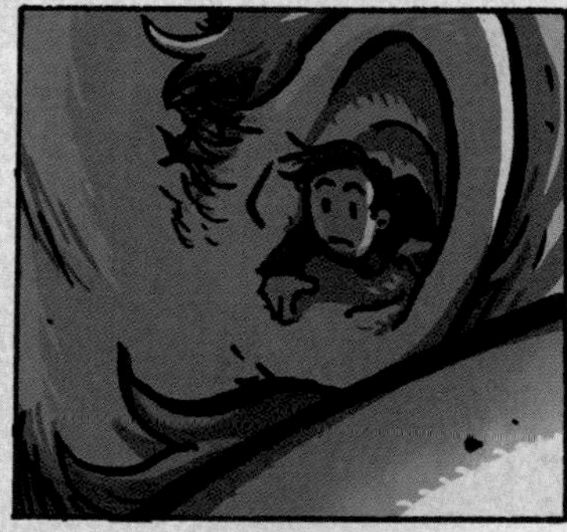

ART
MINI

JUST HAND OVER THE MONEY NICE AND EASY AND KEEP YOUR HANDS RAISED.
HOW DO YOU EXPECT ME TO HAND OVER ANYTHING WHILE MY HANDS—
STOP BEING SUCH A SMART-ASS, OR—
SSHT
KOBASH
KABLAM
SPAK
WHAM
AAA-RRG!
FLIPT
FLIPT
WHAT NOW?
AND WHERE'S CARLOS?
WE CRASHED IN ON A ROBBERY!
DO SOMETHING! JUST TAP ON ANYTHING!

FUMP

MAYBE SOMETHING ELSE!

HEY!
SKIDDDDD

HAT THE—
TAP

FLIP
FLIP

KRAK

ROBERTO, GABRIELLE! AM I GLAD TO SEE YOU!
CARLOS! YOU'RE OKAY!
THE LIGHTS WENT OUT INSIDE! I'M AFRAID WE BROKE HIM!

WELL THERE'S NO TIME TO WORRY ABOUT THAT NOW! THE COP IS COMING, LET'S HIDE IN THE CLIENT'S BACKPOCKET!

FREEZE! THIS IS THE WHAAA?
ARE YOU ALRIGHT, MA'AM? W-WHAT JUST HAPPENED?
SSHHT
IT WAS AMAZING, OFFICER.

THIS HOODED FELLA TRIED TO ROB ME BUT ALL OF A SUDDEN MR. PJ'S HERE RUSHED IN.

THE ROBBER FIRED—BAM! HIT THE COUNTER.
THEN THIS GUY WENT ALL JET LI AND DID THIS CRAZY-ASS KUNG FU THING.

WHACK! CRACK! SNAP, CRACKLE, AND POP, THEY WENT DOWN.
I GOT IT ALL ON TAPE OFFICER.

CAN I PUT MY HANDS DOWN NOW?

MATT, MY LOVE. WE'RE IN A HOSPITAL. YOU LOST CONSCIOUSNESS WHEN YOU TACKLED THE ROBBER LAST NIGHT....

WELL, IT'S A MIRACLE WE DIDN'T GET ANYONE KILLED LAST NIGHT.
HMM.
YEAH.

BUT DO YOU THINK THE BOSS'LL KILL US WHEN SHE HEARS ABOUT OUR INCIDENT?

HARD TO SAY. BUT I DOUBT IT. WE DID ALL RIGHT IN MY OPINION. I MEAN, WE DID MANAGE TO SAVE A CLERK'S LIFE, GET OUR CLIENT'S GIRL BACK, AND APPARENTLY SOLVE HIS MONEY ISSUES. WHO'D HAVE KNOWN THE MINIMART FIGHT WOULD BE AIRED ON THE NEWS?

THE GUY'S PRACTICALLY A CELEBRITY NOW. WITH THAT KIND OF PUBLICITY HE'LL GET ANY ROLE HE'LL WANT.
TRUE.
HE WILL GET THE ROLES HE WANTS.
YOU MIGHT BE RIGHT.

AND WHO ACTUALLY GIVES A RAT'S BEHIND IF WE BRUISED THE CLIENT UP A LITTLE?
DAMN RIGHT!
THE CAUSE JUSTIFIES THE MEANS!

KLAK
KSSSHHHHHHH
I THINK WE HAVE NOTHING TO WORRY ABOUT.

KLAK
KLAK
KLAK

DOCTOR TALBOT. GOOD DAY. YOU HAD A PRETTY NASTY FALL, MR. MOORE, HOW ARE YOU FEELING NOW?
UH, HELLO. OK, I GUESS.

WE TOOK SOME X-RAYS WHILE YOU WERE UN-CONSCIOUS ...
AND?

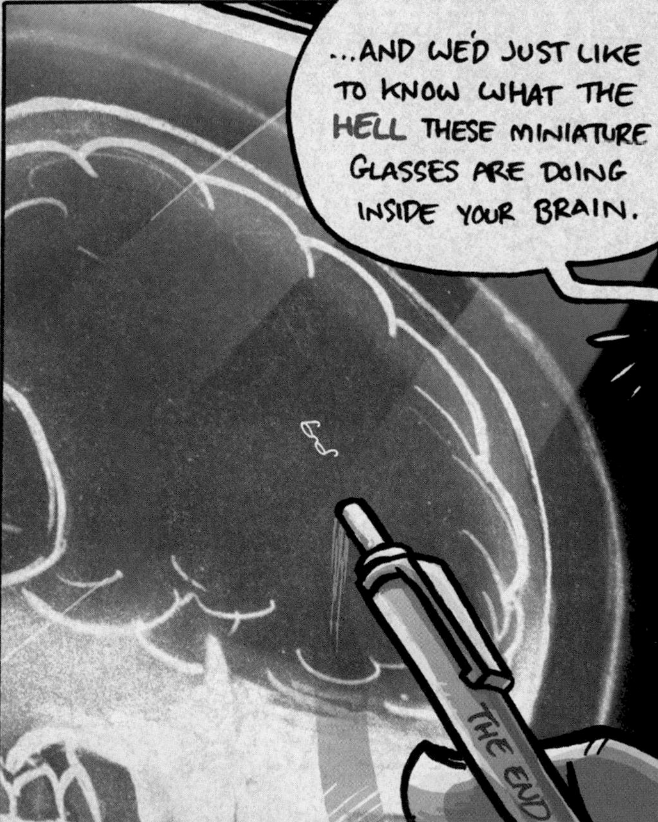
...AND WE'D JUST LIKE TO KNOW WHAT THE HELL THESE MINIATURE GLASSES ARE DOING INSIDE YOUR BRAIN.
THE END

IGLOO Head and Tree Head in Disguise

by: Scott C.

i'll go find treehead. he likes tacos more than war.
holy! what a frightening head!
roaring.
i am just an igloo head. Probably untasty to a dinosaur head.
growling.
JK!
applehead! what the heck?!
where did you get that awesome disguise?
mailordered it.
interesting.
later
dear mailorderhead, please send me an awesome disguise soon. thank you. signed, igloo head
later more
Someone's got a package!
hooray!
O...m...G... it is awesome. time for action.

later again
letter for treehead!
exciting!
dear treehead, i have something important to tell you. meet me by old bridge. signed, suitcase head.
this letter is fishy. i do not know a suitcase head.
gosh. i'm so nervous. i wonder what important thing suitcase head must tell me.
important. that could mean anything. anxious gut.
hello, treehead. i see you have come alone.
suitcasehead. yes. wait. was i supposed to come alone?

i have some pretty incriminating documents inside my head against you, treehead.
and they are official.
oh, man. really?
not really.
igloohead!!
amazing disguise! i want one!
already ordered one for you, "Rockethead"!
no waaa aaaay!
Wow! none of our friends recognize us.
yes. we are completely disguised.
oh, look! there's tankhead. still reading. he disagrees that tacos are delicious.
man. i love tacos.
let's go trick him.
excuse me. we are looking for the war club. have you seen it?
oh, man! yes, it is over there!
thank you. no need for saluting.

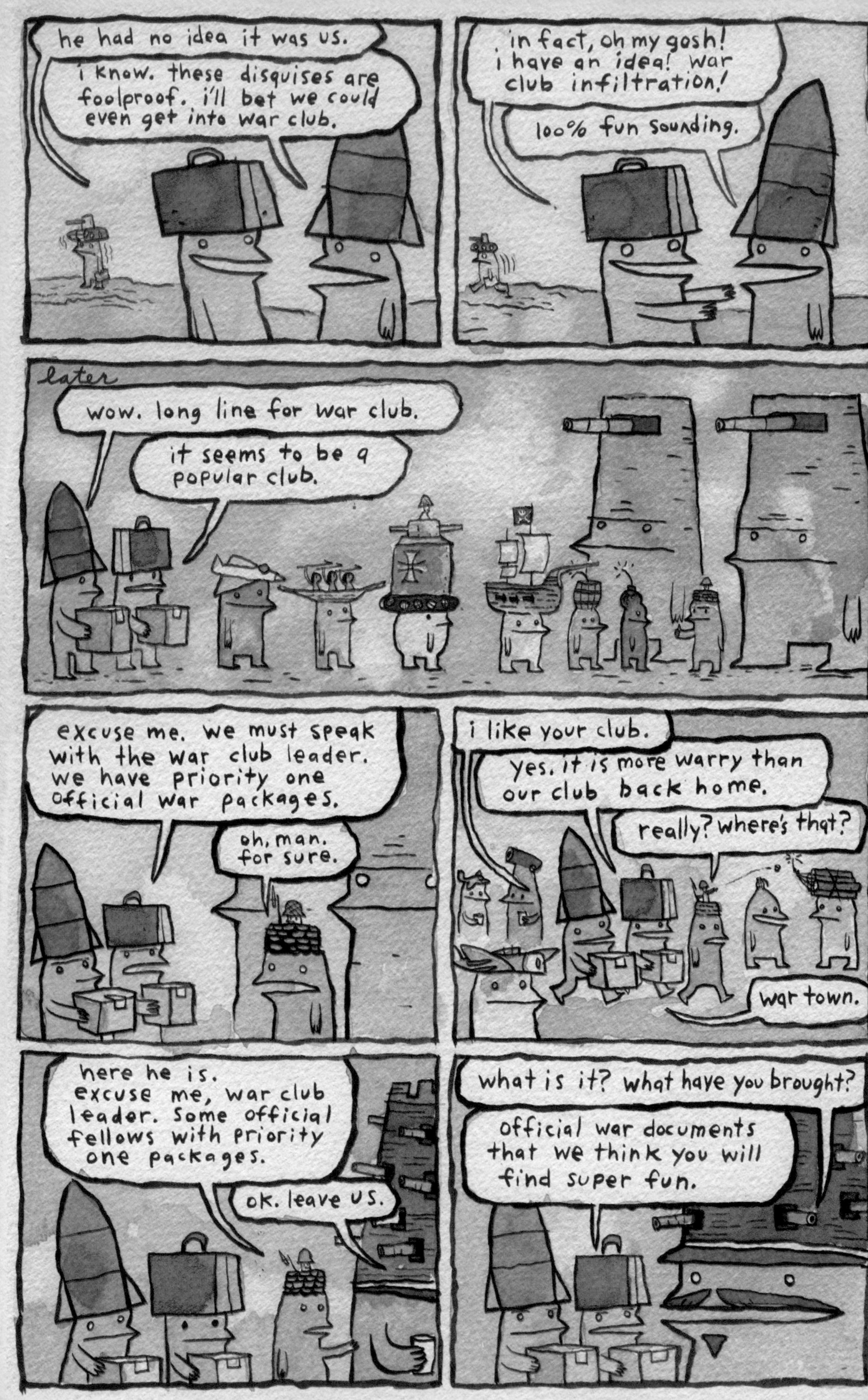
he had no idea it was us.
i know. these disguises are foolproof. i'll bet we could even get into war club.
in fact, oh my gosh! i have an idea! war club infiltration!
100% fun sounding.
later
wow. long line for war club.
it seems to be a popular club.
excuse me. we must speak with the war club leader. we have priority one official war packages.
oh, man. for sure.
i like your club.
yes. it is more warry than our club back home.
really? where's that?
war town.
here he is. excuse me, war club leader. some official fellows with priority one packages.
ok. leave us.
what is it? what have you brought?
official war documents that we think you will find super fun.

hi five

the end.

Evidence.

Be a good boy. Stay in the yard.

BITE!

BITE!

CRASH!

BITE!

Sniff!
Sniff!

Sniff!
Sniff!

Sniff!
Sniff!

Sniff!
Sniff!

Dig!
Dig!

POP!

Gnaw!
Gnaw!

Gnaw!
Gnaw!

Scratch
Scratch!

Come on in.

Oh my God!

Crap!

Dig!
Dig!

Pat!
Pat!
Hammer!
Hammer!

Stay in the yard!
You understand?

Lick!
Lick!

Lick!
Lick!

Oh, you're a good boy!

CRUNCH!

Chew!
Chew!

by
Phil Craven

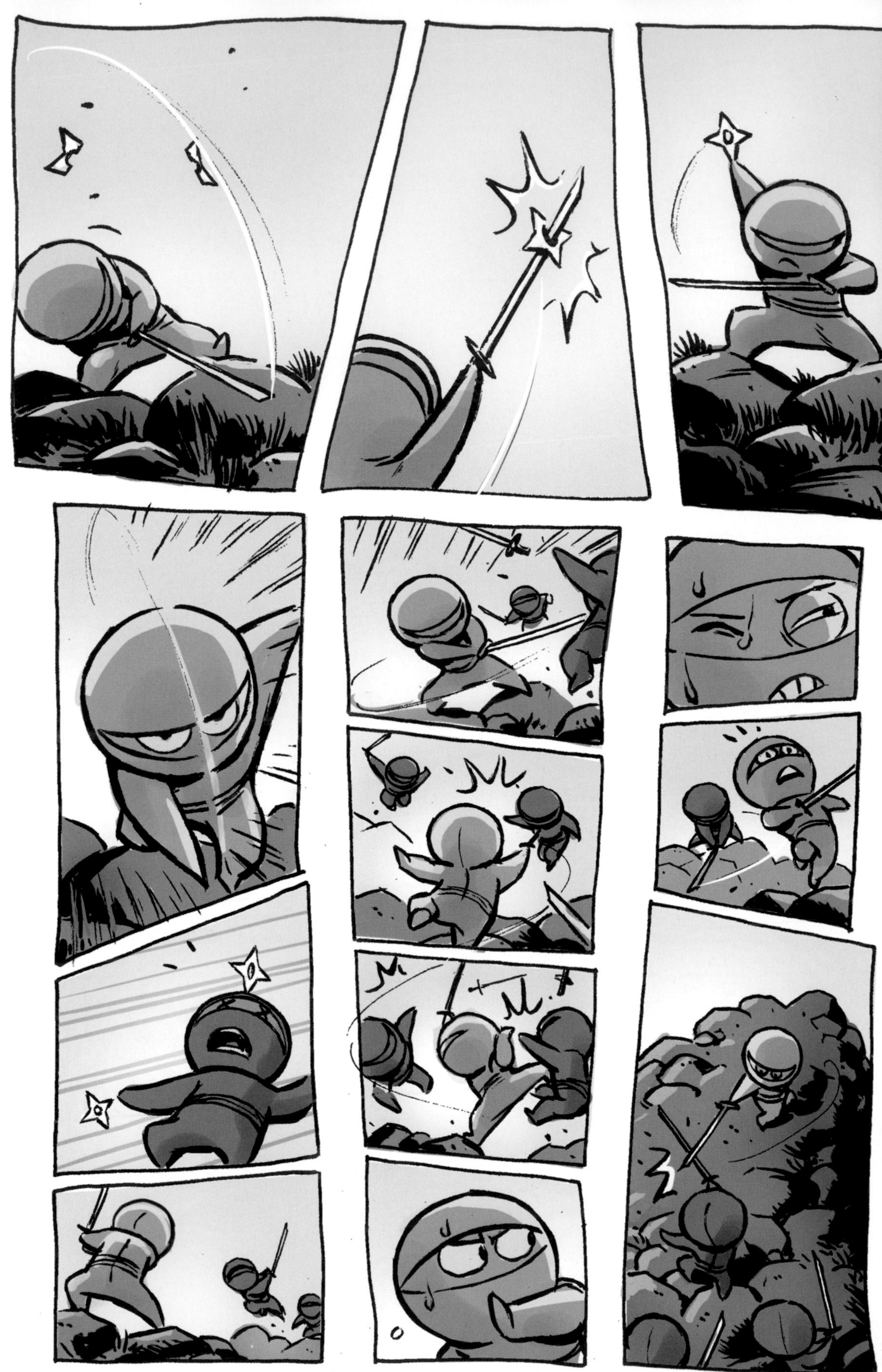

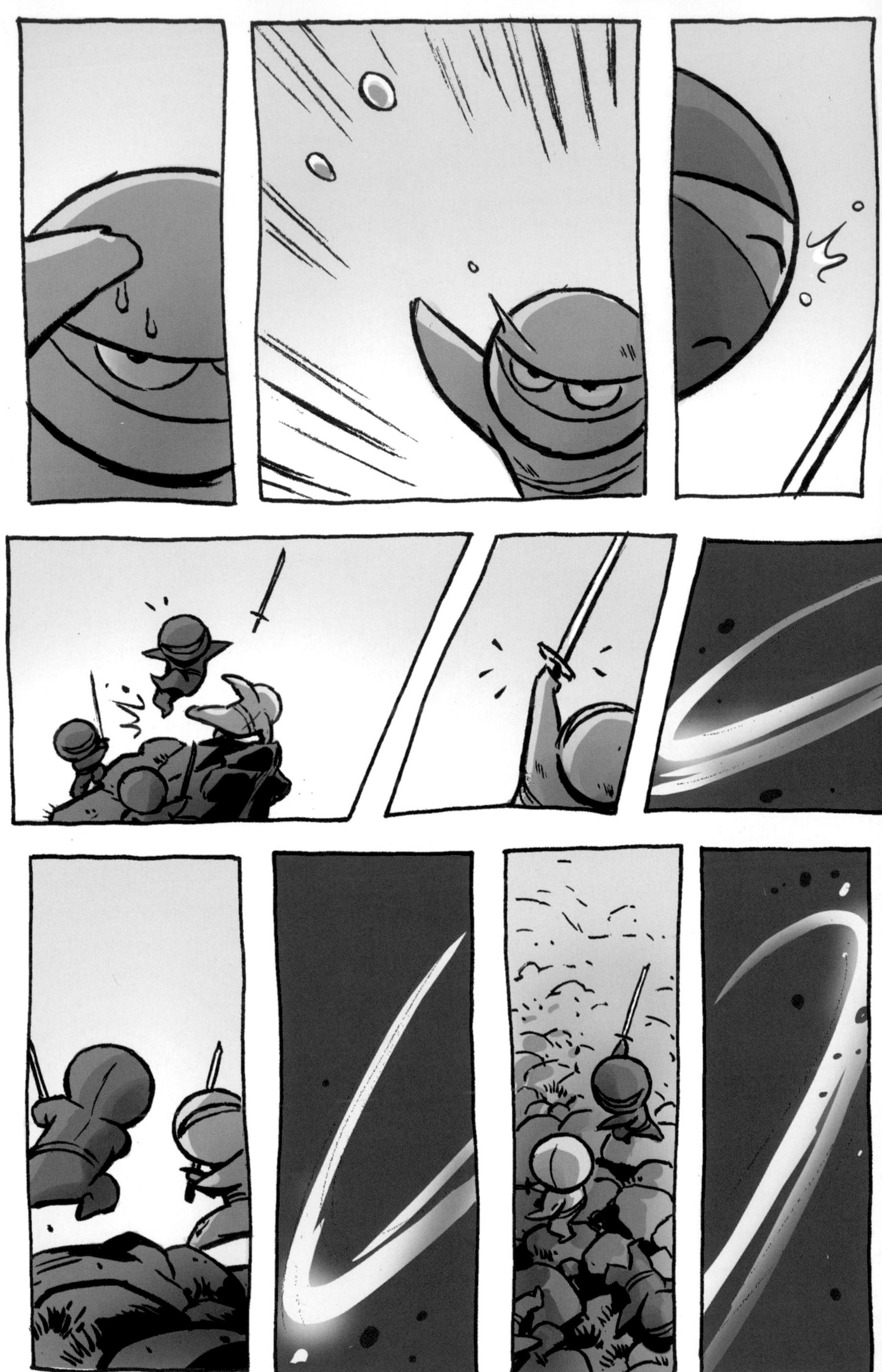

n

THE CHANGELING

OH.
A DEAD FAIRY.
POOR THING...

POOR THING?
I'M GLAD IT'S DEAD.
EVERYONE KNOWS
FAIRIES ARE EVIL.

BY: SARAH MENSINGA

FAIRIES
STEAL
BABIES.

YOU WILL GO AWAY,
BEAR THE CHILD,
AND THEN YOU WILL
RETURN.

WE WILL SAY
YOU ARE OFF
TRAVELING,
VISITING FAMILY.

THE FAIRIES LEAVE A CHANGELING, A FAIRY MONSTER, IN PLACE OF THE BABY AND YOU NEVER GET YOUR BABY BACK.
I'M GONNA BURY IT ANYWAY.
YOU UNDERSTAND YOU CANNOT MARRY HIM.
YOU MUST MARRY WELL.
DON'T WORRY. IT WILL BE AS IF THE CHILD NEVER EXISTED.

NATURALLY, THE INFANT WILL REMAIN HERE IN THE ORPHANGE.
YOU ARE FREE TO WALK THE GROUNDS.
YET NEVER **EVER** ENTER THE FOREST.

WHAT HAVE YOU DONE!? FOOLISH GIRL!
THE FOREST IS INFESTED WITH FAIRIES!

WE MUST KEEP VIGILENT WATCH OVER THE INFANT...

HISSS...

YOUR CHILD WAS TAKEN. SHE IS FOREVER GONE.

THE
END

MOUNTAINS

BY

MATTHEW BERNIER

DEDICATED TO HILARY FLORIDO

THEY WERE THE TWO BIGGEST MOUNTAINS IN THE ISLANDS!

WHERE COULD THEY HAVE GONE?
I DUNNO, BUT THEY'RE NOT HERE.

MAYBE THEY TIPPED OVER.

WE'D HAVE HEARD IT IF THEY'D TIPPED OVER. THEY'D HAVE MADE A HUMONGOUS SPLASH.
THEN I GUESS THEY JUST DISAPPEARED.

THINGS DON'T JUST DISAPPEAR.

WELL...

THEY WERE HERE LAST NIGHT—

AND NOW THEY'RE NOT.
AND NOW THERE'RE ALL THESE MONSTERS INSTEAD.

WHAT'S WITH ALL THESE MONSTERS, ANYHOW?

I DUNNO.
I THINK MAYBE THEY LIVED DEEP DOWN AT THE FEET OF THE MOUNTAINS, AND NOW THEY'VE BEEN ALL STIRRED UP.

THIS IS CREEPING ME OUT.

YEAH.

SAM?
MM?
WE HAVE TO GO.

WHAT?
WE CAN'T STAY HERE. WE HAVE TO FIND ANOTHER ISLAND. SOMEPLACE WITH A MOUNTAIN.

HOW? THERE'S BLOODTHIRSTY MONSTERS ALL AROUND US.
I THINK THEY JUST LOOK SCARY.

WHALES ARE REALLY BIG—BUT THEY'RE FRIENDLY, LIKE PUPPIES!

WHALES DON'T HAVE FIVE-FOOT-LONG FANGS.

WITH THE MOUNTAINS GONE, THERE'LL BE NOTHING TO EAT OR DRINK. THERE'LL BE NO HIGH GROUND TO GO TO IN BIG STORMS.
AND WITH THE HARD PARTS OF THE ISLAND GONE, THE WAVES WILL WASH IT OUT TO SEA, AND US WITH IT.
WE'LL DIE IF WE STAY HERE.
I THINK WE SHOULD WAIT.
WHAT IF THEY COME BACK WITHOUT US?
WE'D FEEL REALLY DUMB IF THEY REAPPEARED WITH US FIFTY MILES OUT.
AND WE HAVE HURRICANE RATIONS FOR SIX WEEKS.

OKAY, WE'LL WAIT.

GOOD NIGHT, SAM.
GOOD NIGHT, FIL.

SAM, WE CAN'T KEEP WAITING. THE MONSTERS' SCRAPING UP AGAINST THE SHORE IS GRINDING THE ISLAND AWAY.

I'VE BEEN TRYING SOMETHING WHILE YOU'VE BEEN SLEEPING.

WATCH THIS!
WHAT ARE—

FIL, NO!!
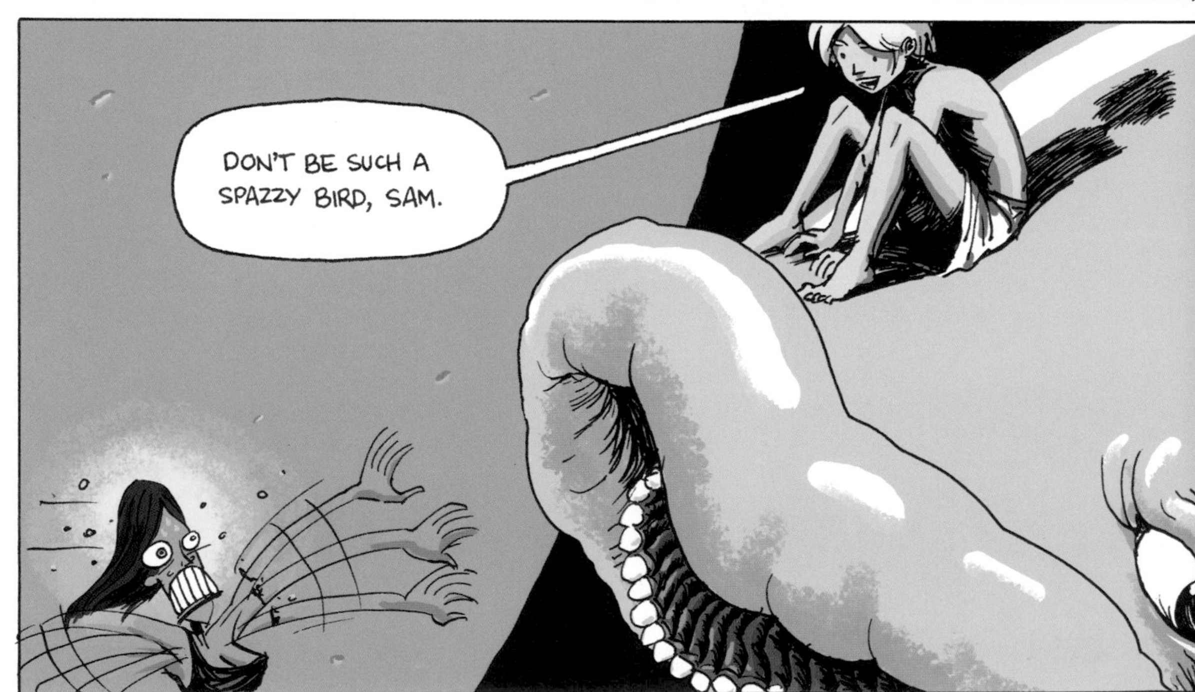
DON'T BE SUCH A SPAZZY BIRD, SAM.

SEE? THEY'RE HARMLESS! WE CAN WALK ON THEIR BACKS TO THE NEXT ISLAND!

I DON'T THINK SO.

I'VE ALWAYS BEEN AFRAID OF DEEP WATER, CAUSE I'D IMAGINE HORRIBLE THINGS I COULDN'T SEE LOOKING UP AT ME, WAITING TO GRAB ME AND PULL ME INTO THE DARKNESS.

WELL, WE HAVE TO GO SOMEWHERE. THERE'S NOT MUCH "HERE" LEFT FOR US TO STAY.

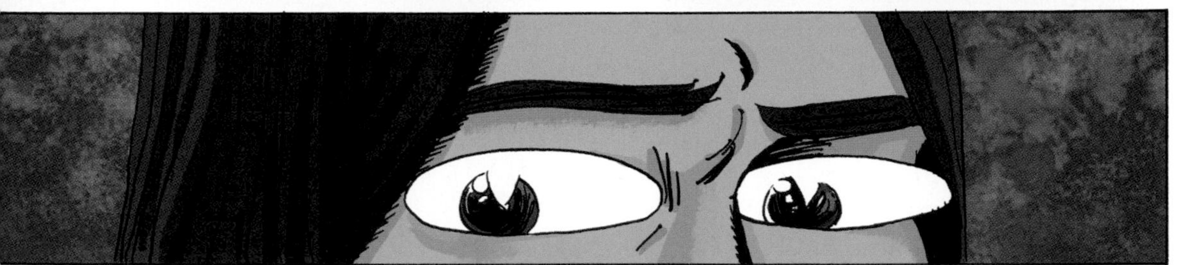

I'LL TAKE THE BOAT.
AT LEAST THERE'LL BE A FLOOR BETWEEN ME AND THEM.

OKAY, THEN.

ARE YOU READY?
NO.

I CAN FEEL THEIR SCALES SCRAPING THE BOTTOM...

WA!

AH...

C'MERE, SILLY.

THAT'S IT, GET YOUR FEET IN ITS CHIN PLEATS!

THIS IS...
IT'S REALLY HARD TO KEEP MY FOOTING.
BUT YOU CAN STAND UP NOW, RIGHT?

C'MON, LET'S START WALKING.

WHAT HAPPENS IF THE MOUNTAIN ON OUR NEW ISLAND DISAPPEARS?
THEN WE'LL KNOW WHAT TO DO, AND IT WON'T BE SO SCARY.

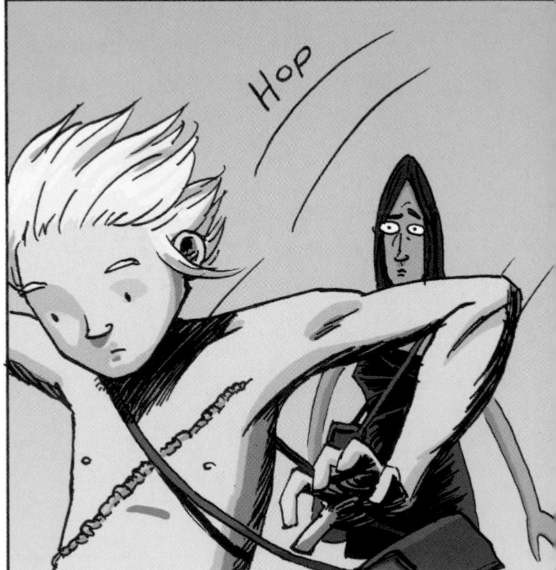

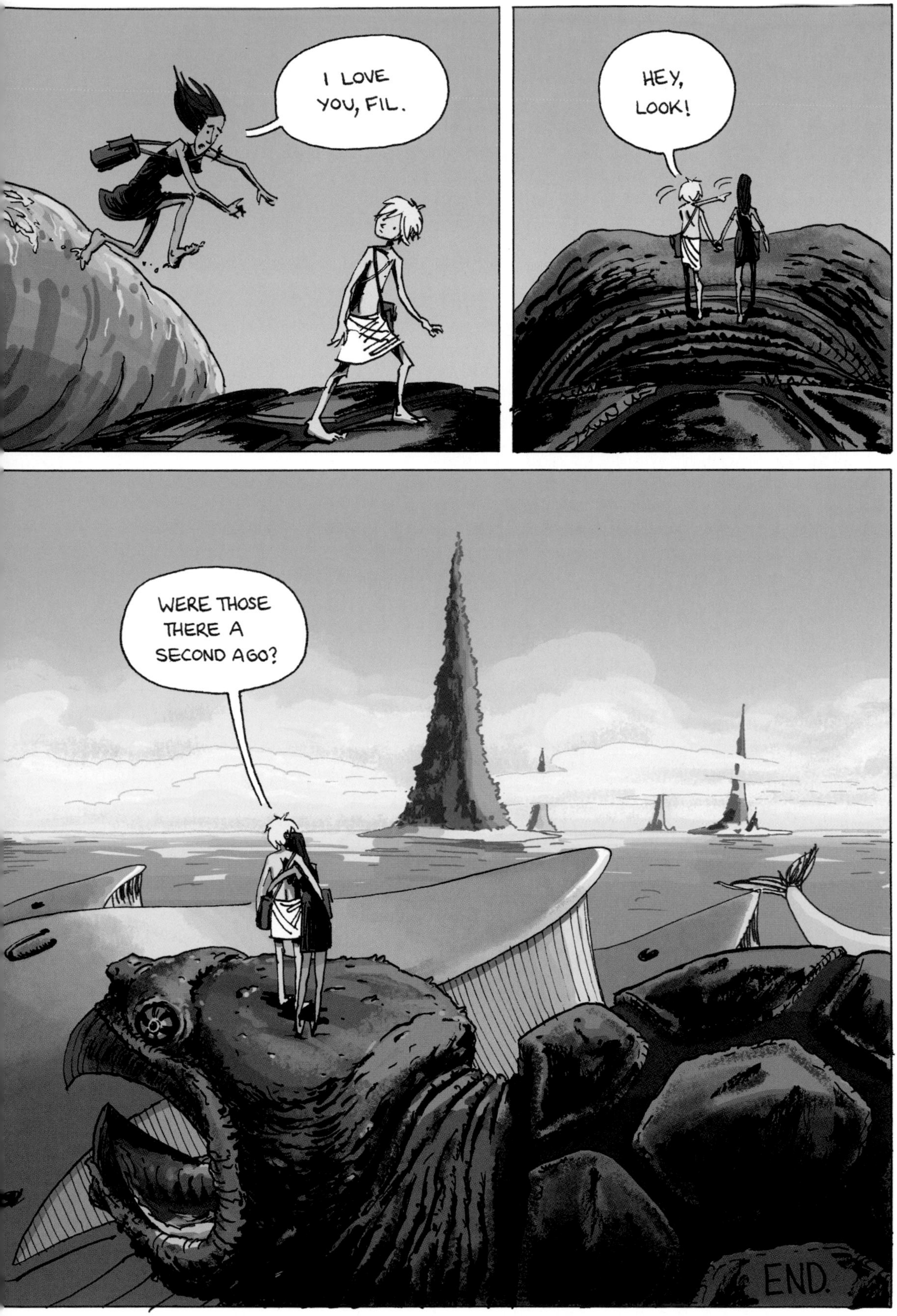

WERE THOSE THERE A SECOND AGO?

END.

AND THEY CALLED ME...

BIGDOME

The Aeronautical Adventures of Myles Preston Thackerly III

"FLOWERS for MAMA"

As dutifully related by: Paul Rivoche

SPUT SPUT
VRNNNNN
LOOK! One of our KITES— IN TROUBLE!!

VRAAWWW
But WHO?? None of the fellows are up—
He's going to make a BELLY LANDING!

!
SSCREEEKKKKK
KTUNGGG
ow!

—cough— GOOD LORD! It's the THACKERLY lad! What's it all about, cadet?
459
—OWW-W— Oh Mama, it aches fiercely— ARGH—alert the Air Ministry— the brute is DEAD—

Royal Helmonautical Academy, Sunday 15th March '08

Dear Mama, I'm dreadfully sorry I've been so tardy with my correspondence and am very late with these birthday greetings! You see, I've been quite laid up for two weeks in the infirmary—after a rather nasty tumble in my machine...

SKRIT
SKRITCH
The tale of my infirmity began thusly: I had a notion that—as a token of your great value to me—I would procure for you something **delicate** and **exotic**, as a fitting **birthday gift!**

But the question was, **HOW**? I began by means of diligent research in the school library.

All avenues seemed closed to me, when some of the sturdier lads of our institution chanced upon my plight.
OY!
PSSST...WOT'S BIGDOME UP TO??

Soon, one of these stout fellows unselfishly loaned me a family heirloom: a **hand-drawn** aeronautical chart!

Retiring to my quarters, I studied it with all possible enthusiasm...

...And early the next morning, whilst the other pupils slumbered, I took to the skies.
459

The document pinpointed the **secret** location of **RARE, HIGH-ALTITUDE FLOWERS!**

To gain my prize, I was obliged to push my venerable steed above its service ceiling...

Arriving at the coordinates indicated on the chart, my mount bucking in the thin air, I found–
NOTHING!
The first doubts about the document's veracity began to trickle into my mind, when–

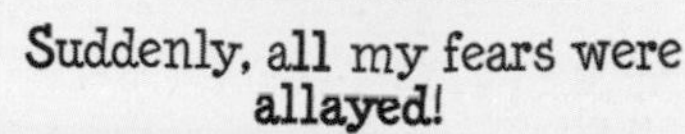
Suddenly, all my fears were **allayed!**

459
!

For—above me was the promised **ISLAND OF FLOWERS!**

Oddly, upon closer inspection, it appeared to be a **derelict hulk** of some sort. Not a likely spot for a **flower meadow**...yet, I pressed on, as the lads had promised **SAT-IS-FACTION!**

HMFS ARIES

With an exultant heart
I ascended, seeking
an entryway...
...and soon,
my prayers
were answered!

Inside the dome, a miniature **Eden** awaited me!

I will forever remember the glorious hour which I passed
that afternoon–there, in that sunlit valley of the most
exquisite **rarity**...
I harvested a brimming
satchelful of precious
beauties for **you**, Mama....

But alas, my reverie
was destined to be
interrupted–

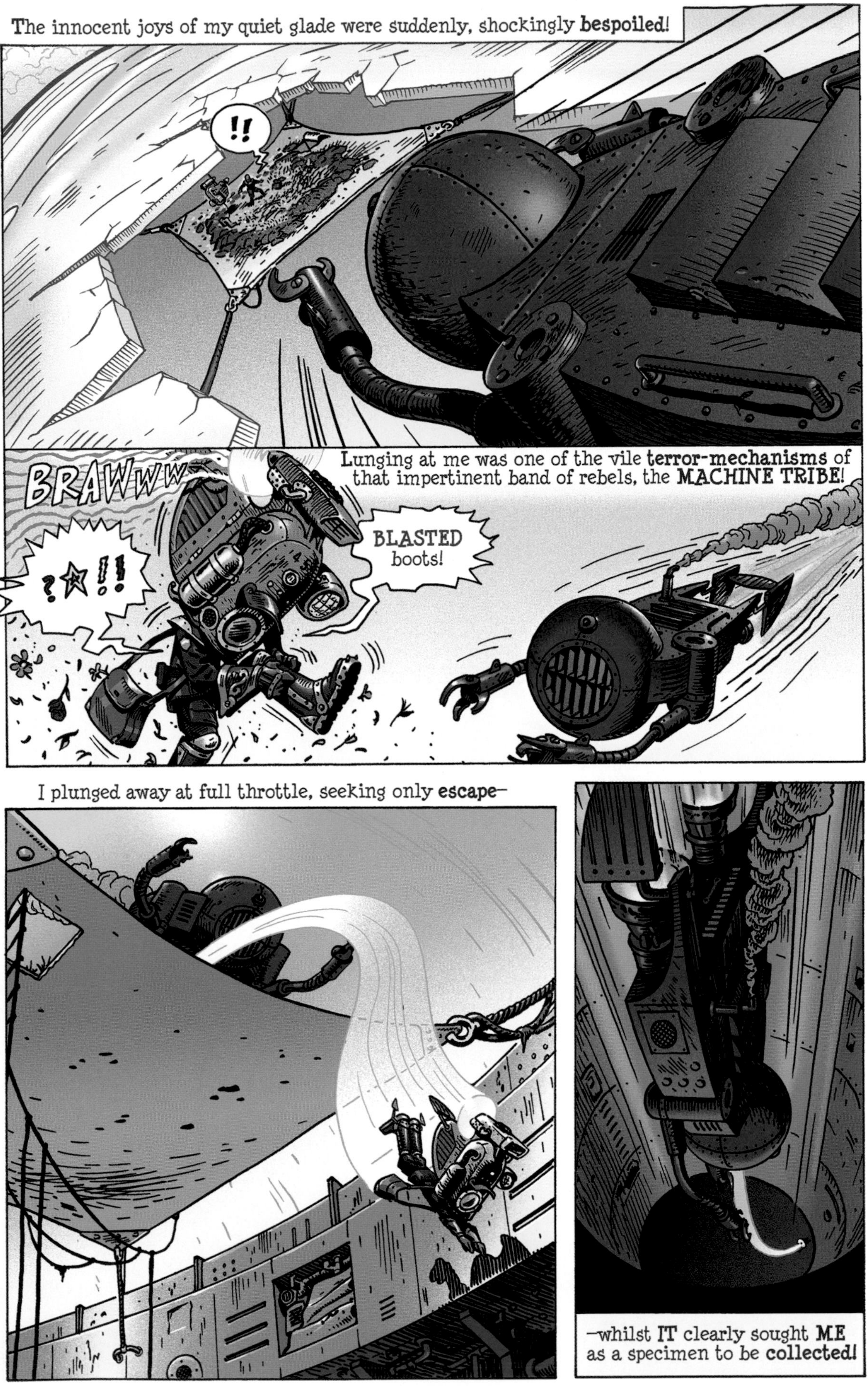

The innocent joys of my quiet glade were suddenly, shockingly **bespoiled**!

!!

BRAWWW

Lunging at me was one of the vile **terror-mechanisms** of that impertinent band of rebels, the **MACHINE TRIBE**!

?☆!!

BLASTED boots!

I plunged away at full throttle, seeking only **escape**—

—whilst **IT** clearly sought **ME** as a specimen to be **collected**!

For a brief moment I **eluded** my foul pursuer, the **machine beast**–

But in a moment it **beset** me once more!–

I felt its **iron doom** upon me, Mother...and I knew what I **must** do–

With **desperate** tears, I fumbled for my satchel—and for one last **wild hope!**

Perhaps you will someday forgive me, Mother—but–
I selfishly **sacrificed** your bouquet, that day, on the altar of **dire necessity!**

My propeller did its ugly work—eagerly generating a swirling **flower-miasma** which **filled** the tunnel–
rGGGGNNAWWW

And then at last—THE LIGHT!

An ominous **clanging** inside the shaftway signified the beast's DEATH-RATTLE!

Although my machine was given to dive like a brute, it still could not outrun the fantastic SHOCK WAVE generated by the death of the **entire vessel**!

K-K-ROOOMMM

I was about to fix my course for home, when—

AAAAAAAAA

?

In short order, I was forced to **deposit** this vexacious beggar upon the nearest peak, to make his **own** way home!

I then grew quite **cheery**! —fondly reflecting upon the **decoration** I'll surely receive from the **Air Ministry**, for my **attack** and **destruction** of the enemy drone!

Just then, however, my engine lost **all** pressure...

...so I thought it **prudent** to make my landing.

Oh–I must tell you–a few minutes ago the fellows came by. Seems they'd just met with **headmaster** & were quite **downcast**...
Thackerly...um...we–do **APOLOGIZE**–
Apologize, **rubbish**! I should be the one grovelling, for losing your **crown jewel**!

Gosh, that map was **SPOT ON**! I'd be **ever** so grateful if you'd consider lending me **another** one!
They promised to loan me another one by summer hols!

Enclosed are your hard-won flowers, Mama. Please **do** ask Father to watch the papers closely: my name should figure prominently any day now. In closing–
Excuse me, Mr. Thackerly, but it's time for your **vitamin** series.
Mrs. Edmond Thackerly
5 Churchill Lane

There's also a **telegram**, and the **newspaper** you asked for.

Telegram! I say! SPLENDID! The Air Ministry **FINALLY** responded!

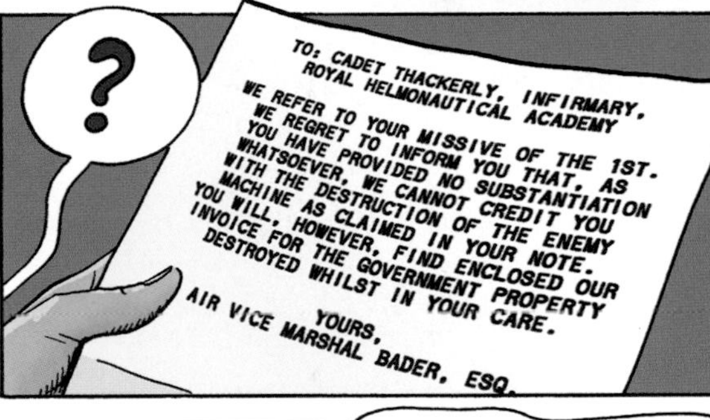
?
TO: CADET THACKERLY, INFIRMARY, ROYAL HELMONAUTICAL ACADEMY
WE REFER TO YOUR MISSIVE OF THE 1ST. WE REGRET TO INFORM YOU THAT, AS YOU HAVE PROVIDED NO SUBSTANTIATION WHATSOEVER, WE CANNOT CREDIT YOU WITH THE DESTRUCTION OF THE ENEMY MACHINE AS CLAIMED IN YOUR NOTE. YOU WILL, HOWEVER, FIND ENCLOSED OUR INVOICE FOR THE GOVERNMENT PROPERTY DESTROYED WHILST IN YOUR CARE.
YOURS,
AIR VICE MARSHAL BADER, ESQ.

Some minutes later–
ohhh–T-THIS IS JUST A HORROR–
Well, just cease your snivelling and **clenching**, then! It's only **ten small pinches**!
THE DAILY OPTIC
DHALGREN TRIUMPHS
'Aries' Sole Survivor Awarded Meda
GREAT HONOR.
Order of The Ironclad Rarely Bestowed: Hero Dhalgren Fought 5-Day Battle against Machine Beast.
MANDER SEEKS RETURN TO FLORICULTURE.

Mr. Thackerly, I declare, you must **BRAVEN UP** quite substantially if you hope to someday emulate the **heroics** of that Captain Dhalgren the broadsheets are **ALL** speaking of!
JAB!
AAAAAARGHH
END

This Morning I Woke up to discover that I was
The Chosen One
Chosen for WHAT, exactly?
LOS KNIGHTS
As told by:
Dave Roman
With help from Raina

The Prophecy

You will save t
world from grea
peril. There shall
be a quest in which
you shall receive a tool
of usefulness which

SQUEE?

NO...I DON'T want the world to end. SHEESH...Way to guilt-trip a guy.
SQUAWK!
OKAY, OKAY. I'll keep reading.

boon to all
Time of reckoning in
Forbidden Forest etc.
Key to unlock doorway
of enlightenment.
is a guardian
a hero
Are you sure I'm the only one who can do this?

You made me a T-shirt?
THE CHOSEN ONE
I see...

BAHH!
Yeah. I'm TOTALLY gonna wear it.
THE CHOSEN ONE

But is it okay if I take a shower first?
THE CHOSEN ONE

When I got to school, everything seemed fairly normal.
THE CHOSEN ONE

Hey, Amy. Notice anything DIFFERENT about me?
THE CHOSEN ONE

Anything worth SINGLING out? That SEPARATES me from the rest of common society?
You're covered in animal dander?
THE CHOSEN ONE

Yes.
Yes I AM.
PAT PAT
THE CHOSEN ONE

STUPID WOODLAND CREATURES!
THE CHOSEN ONE

But minutes later...
HOLY SMOKES! Look at that T-shirt!
GASP
THE CHOSEN ONE
Is it TRUE?!
Has he really RETURNED TO US?!
THE CHOSEN ONE
Well, according to the prophecy...
HE QUOTES THE SACRED TEXTS!
AND THUS I KNEEL BEFORE HIM!!!
THE CHOSEN ONE
MAN, I hope some cute girls are watching this.
HOW MAY WE SERVE YOU!?
WE HAVE BEEN WAITING FOR YOUR ARRIVAL!
THE CHOSEN ONE

During lunch...
Here is your second helping of dessert, Chosen One.
Mmm.
I'm done drawing the map!
?
School
secret tunnel
Supermarket
You're gonna want to take the secret tunnel behind the Stop 'n' Shop.
That's the fastest way to the Forbidden Forest.
Are you SURE I should be going to the Forbidden Forest?
Yeah. Why?
Cuz it's FORBIDDEN, maybe?
THE CHOSEN ONE
I see your point. But that's never stopped anyone before.
THE CHOSEN ONE
And since you're the Chosen One, it's like an ALL-ACCESS pass.

So, after classes...
Is this your first time in a secret tunnel?
Yeah, can you tell?
NAH.
Okay. This is it.
We've reached THE THRESHOLD!
You'll have to journey the rest of the way by YOURSELF.
Thanks for all your help.
THE CHOSEN ONE
LESS SCARY
MORE SCARY

WAIT! Don't bother to bring your backpack. You won't need it in THERE.
Oh.
THE CHOSEN ONE

I feel kind of naked in here without it.

But at least I got this T-shirt!
THE CHOSEN ONE

Oh, hey! There's SOME BUNNY.
I wonder if he's hip to this Quest business.
HEY, SCOTT! I've been waiting for you.
THE CHOSEN ONE

NUTS! Am I reading your mind?
Yup! Since bunnies don't make any sounds, we must communicate telepathically.
RIGHT ON!
THE CHOSEN ONE
So, whatcha got for me?
This is The Key.
Looks like a weapon. Is it magic?
It opens the DOOR OF POSSIBILITIES.
I LIKE IT!
SWOOOSH!

So with key in hand, I ventured further through the dark wood...
THE CHOSEN ONE
MARCH
MARCH
...and fought many potential dangers.
AHHHH!
GASP!
Surrounded by GHASTS!

AAAAAAAAHHH!

ZIP

LEAP
SHEESH!

THE CHOSEN ONE
YEAH! You'd **BETTER** run!

WOW! I didn't realize I had that in me.
Maybe those animals were **RIGHT!**

I better go save the world...
...while I'm still **BUZZED!**

It wasn't long before I found the door in question. And I wasn't the only one.

Scott?

YOU SUCK!
Now I totally have to fight you!
It doesn't have to go down like this!
THE CHOSEN ONE
There can only be ONE!
CLANG
CLASH
DON'T BE SO SURE!!
CLANG

WHAT?! Please don't tell me my ex-girlfriend is on a Quest, too!
I'm the champion of the people.
And her key has a cute ribbon tied to it.
Yeah, I GUESS that's pretty neat.

Now what? I don't really feel like a fight to the finish.
We could... team up.
THE CHOSEN ONE
THE CHOSEN ONE
THE CHOSEN ONE

But if I'M the Chosen One...and you're ALSO the Chosen One...and Britta's the Chosen One AS WELL...
Then we'll call ourselves...
THE CHOSEN ONE

1

THE CHOSEN ONES CLUB FOR THE CHOSEN FEW

Let's open this door and stop that monster before it's too late.
On the count of three!

No! Counting down. Three...two...
...ONE.

What's inside?
I'm not sure...
THE CHOSEN ONE
Looks like nothing.

You mean this is just an empty hallow tree?
No, wait! LOOK CLOSER!

HEY! There's POPCORN inside!
OOH! I could SO go for some of that!
POP CORN

So we came all the way out here just for snacks?
I'm not complaining.
Me neither.
HEY! What are you kids doing UP THERE?!
THE CHOSEN ONE
POP CORN

Don't you know it's dangerous to play in a Haunted Forest?
THE CHOSEN ONE
A WIZARD!

Close. I'm actually the forest RANGER.
This woodland is a preserve that you're trespassing on.

But I'm—I mean, WE are supposed to be here to stop the END OF THE WORLD!
Oh, that? Steve handled that last week.
Steve? WHO'S STEVE?!

Just some RANDOM DUDE.
He came down here, picked the lock with a paperclip, and beat up the monster inside, thus stopping the impending doom.
POW
But the T-SHIRTS!
And the KEYS!
And my BIRTHMARK!
#1
Sounds like the animals have fallen off the wagon again.
Once they sink their teeth into a prophecy they can't let go. It's like an addiction. They're probably off silk-screening more shirts as we speak.
So no one chose Steve to be the only person who could save the world?
Nope. He just had the afternoon free.

Where does that Steve guy get off stealing our thunder?
I CHOOSE not to believe it.
STOMP STOMP

Besides, being the ONLY ONES who can save the world is kind of played out.
So then what do you want to do now?
THE CHOSEN ONE

The next day, at Steve's house...
DING DONG!
Joseph Campbell's MYTH SOUP
RADIO
FANBOY

Are you Steve?
Who's asking?
YOUR CLEVER AND FUNNY SIDEKICKS!!!
WELCOME

And so...
GO GET 'EM, STEVE!
WE'RE BEHIND YOU ALL THE WAY!
DANGER

THE END!

"LOST"

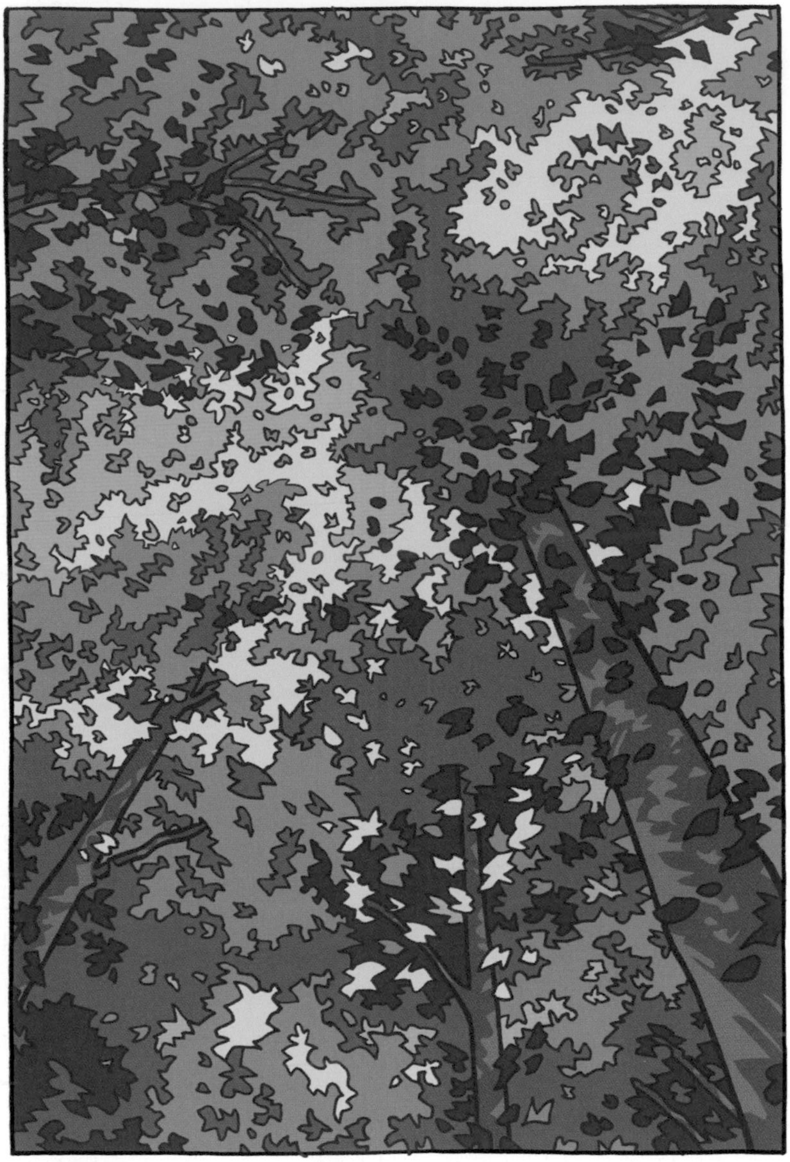

KEAN SOO

WE'RE LOST!!

I KNEW IT! I KNEW IT! I TOLD YOU WE SHOULDN'T HAVE WANDERED OFF THE PATH!

WHAT ARE WE GONNA DO? WHAT ARE WE GONNA DO?

IT'LL BE YEARS BEFORE THEY EVEN FIND OUR SKELETONS!

OKAY, MAYBE IT WASN'T THE BRIGHTEST MOVE ON MY PART, BUT WE CAN'T PANIC IF WE WANT TO GET OUT OF HERE.

BESIDES, WE SHOULD AT LEAST ENJOY OURSELVES INSTEAD OF WORRYING SO MUCH.

APPRECIATE THE SIGHTS WHILE WE'RE OUT HERE, YOU KNOW?

THANKS.

WELL.

SEE? THERE'S THE RIVER. ALL WE NEED TO DO NOW IS FOLLOW THAT BACK TO THE PARK ENTRANCE. EASY.

HA HA HA! WE'RE SAVED! SAVED!!

THANK YOU THANK YOU

BOYS.

WELL, I SUPPOSE IT'S A GOOD THING WE FOUND THIS WHEN WE DID.

FOR A MINUTE THERE, EVEN *I* WAS STARTING TO WORRY THAT WE'D NEVER FIND THE RIVER EITHER.

!

YOU COMING, JELLABY?

Two Kids

Story
Grimaldi

Art
Bannister

Colors
Steve Hamaker

Mummyyyy ?

Daddyyyyy ?

BWAAAHH...

Oh, shut up !
You're deafening me !

If your parents don't hear you when you shout, they won't hear you when you cry either.

You're lost too ?
No. I'm just hiding.

From what ?
From my parents.

Why ?

Because they're going to divorce.

What's your name ?
Sarah. Yours ?
Paul.

FRTT!!
SCHHFF!

FRT
FRRT
FRT
FRT FRTT

...

BWAAAHH...

Relax !
I was hiding in case
it was my parents.
Stop whining !

You don't want
to see your parents
ever ?
I do.
But not yet.
I want them
to be scared
a little.

I wish I was
with my parents.
But I don't
even know
where
the path is.
What am I
gonna do ?

Do you have
anything
to eat ?

I have cookies.
Cool !
Give them
to me !

No way ! I must save them if I have to live in the forest.

You're stupid.
OK. You give them to me, and I tell you how to find the path.

OK. I'm listening.

It's quite simple. Take a look at this place, and fetch it into your mind. Then, choose a direction, and walk straight.

After a moment, if you don't find the path, just come back straight here.

One direction after another, you'll find the path.

I didn't find it.
Try another direction.

Grimaldi – Bannister – Hamaker 2008

SUDDENLY!

SCENES IN WHICH THE EARTH STOPS SPINNING AND EVERYBODY FLIES INTO A WALL

WRITTEN BY RYAN NORTH DRAWN BY JOHN MARTZ

GO LONG!
THOK!
SUDDENLY!
AWESOME!
REX
2

SUDDENLY!

Jenn's
BUFFET SPECIAL
ALL YOU CAN EAT

I FORGOT THE FORTUNE COOKIES!

SUDDENLY!
TAKE ONLY WHAT YOU CAN EAT

TRACK
MEET
TODAY

ON YOUR MARKS...
GET SET...
GO!
BANG!!

SUDDENLY!

AND SO IF THERE IS ANYONE HERE WHO KNOWS A REASON WHY THESE TWO SHOULD NOT BE WED...
LET THEM SPEAK NOW...
OR FOREVER HOLD THEIR PEACE.
CHECK OUT THE STAINED-GLASS WINDOW!
MAN, IMAGINE IF IT GOT SMASHED SOMEHOW.
THEN I NOW PRONOUNCE YOU HUSBAND AND WIFE
THAT WOULD BE SWEET.
CLAP CLAP CLAP

SUDDENLY!

THE END.

TIMECAT
by JOEY WEISER
TIME
JUMP INTO
THE FUTURE!

HMF!

EDDIE...
9:56
FEED ME!
PURR
FEED ME!
PURR

YOU KNOW WE FEED YOU AT 11:00...
9:56
NOW, BE GOOD.

AAARGH!!!! SO UNFAIR!
HE JUST EATS WHENEVER HE LIKES!!

THIS LEAVES ME NO CHOICE... BUT TO USE... IT...

I MUST USE MY SECRET POWER, AS "TIMECAT"...
...TO JUMP INTO THE FUTURE!

9:57

CONCENTRATE...
FOCUS...

NNNGRRGGH!
wiggle
wiggle

AH!

9:58

RATS! NOT FAR ENOUGH... IT'S NO USE... I DON'T HAVE COMPLETE CONTROL OF MY POWERS YET...

I'LL JUST HAVE TO DO THIS THE OLD-FASHIONED WAY...

FEED ME!
PURR
PURR

COMICS
DEVIL DINO
DEVIL DINO

FEED ME FEED ME FEED ME FEED ME FEED ME FEED ME FEED ME FEED ME FEED ME FEED ME FEED ME FEED ME FEED ME FEED ME
PURR PURR

EDDIE. BE GOOD.
COMICS
DEVIL DINO
DEVIL DINO

...MEDITATE...RELAX...THINK OF THE FUTURE...BOY THIS LAP SURE IS...COMFY...

Z

WHAT THE—?
WHERE AM I!?!

THAT'S RIGHT! I WAS JUMPING INTO THE FUTURE!
WHAT TIME IS IT??

11:22

11:22...?
TH-THAT'S...PAST MY FEEDING TIME!

I'VE JUMPED...TOO FAR!!

NOOOOOOOOO!!!!
Z

Zznx---huh?

snivel
weep

HEY EDDIE...

IT'S TIME TO FEED YOU!
ISN'T IT?
!

THE DAY IS SAVED!
THE END

VOYAGE
ART
KNESS & MADE

"ON THE IMPORTANCE OF SPACE TRAVEL"

by Svetlana Chmakova

(toning help: Sasha Chmakova)

SO FOR MY SHOW & TELL I WILL BE TALKING ABOUT WHAT IT'S LIKE TO LIVE ON PLUTO.

...AND, AND BE A PRINCESS.

...

I DON'T HAVE ANY PHOTOS...

...BECAUSE THEY GOT VACUUM-DAMAGED WHEN WE GOT HIT BY THAT ASTEROID...

NO, DUH.

NATHAN, QUIET.

DID THE ASTEROID HIT YOU IN THE HEAD, TOO?

NATHAN!

HA HA HA

NO, NO, WE WERE ALL FINE, WE JUST LOST SOME BOXES.

BUT I DREW SOME PICTURES!
THIS WAS OUR WINTER PALACE
AND THIS WAS MY TIARA.
THERE WAS OCEAN RIGHT UNDER MY BALCONY...
AND I MADE FRIENDS WITH THE ICE MERMAIDS.
... OH, AND THIS!
THIS IS FROM OUR CAMPING TRIP ON MARS!
IT WAS SO DUSTY THERE, I HAD TO WEAR A BIOFIELD.
THIS THING.
... AND THIS WAS MY TIARA. BUT IT MELTED.

I ALSO HAVE THESE ROCKS FROM SAT...
RRING
SCHOOL'S OUT!
YAY!

...EVERYONE, DON'T FORGET YOUR PERMISSION SLIPS FOR THE FIELDTRIP!
...NATHAN, THAT BARETTE'S NOT YOURS, GIVE IT BACK!
OH, IT'S DONE...

...YOUR ROCK WAS SO AWESOME, CAN I HOLD IT?
FIVE BUCKS, HAHA!
UM, BYE!

...
♪

...I WILL NEED TO SPEAK TO YOUR FATHER, JEANNIE. AGAIN.
OH, OKAY, I'LL TELL HIM!

?

...HI,
NATHAN.

AH!!
HEY, YOUR
NEPTUNE HIGHNESS
SWIM IN
THIS!
HA HA
HA
HA

IT'S
PLUTO!
HA
HA
HA HA

WIPE
WIPE

HI, SPACE GIRL.
HI, MRS. FLETCHER!

......!!

TO: JEANNIE GON
27 SUNSET

HAHA, FAIR ENOUGH!

YAY YAY YAY YAY

JEANNIE

PLOP!
TWIST
TWIST
OHH...

BLAH
BLAH
BLAH
...SERIOUSLY?!
PLUTO CRYSTALS?
WHAT ARE ALL THESE SYMBOLS?
DOES IT DO ANYTHING?
IT'S A PERSONAL NAVIGATION DEVICE.
FOR, FOR WHEN YOU ARE FLYING IN THE CLOUDS AND CAN'T SEE WHERE YOU ARE GOING.
YANK!
AH!
SO, WHAT, YOU CAN FLY NOW?
...UM, I ALWAYS COULD.
HI, NATHAN.
HEY, I WONDER IF YOU CAN TALK TO URANUS ON THIS!
PLUTO!
EARTH TO URANUS, COME IN URANUS! WE GOT YOUR ALIEN HERE!

PLEASE GIVE IT BACK!
COME AND GET IT, YOUR PLUTO HIGHNESS!
TOSS
URANUS!!
...I MEAN...
HA HA HA HA
NATHAN!! STOP THAT!!
RRSTLE
...NOT A PROBLEM FOR SOMEONE WHO CAN FLY, RIGHT?

?
CRRUNCH

SEVERAL WEEKS LATER.

RRRING

HEE HEE

HI, GUYS, LONG TIME NO SEE! WHAT ARE YOU...
STAY AWAY FROM US, YOU PSYCHO!!

I'M NOT A...
DO YOU UNDERSTAND ENGLISH?!
STAY AWAY!!

LET'S GO OVER THERE.

VISITING HOURS
MON-FRI 6:00-8:00 p.m.
SAT-SUN 4:00-5:00 p.m.

...

...

SIGH

IT...
IT WASN'T
MY FAULT!!
SHE'S
CRAZY!

SHE THINKS
SHE'S FROM
PLUTO!

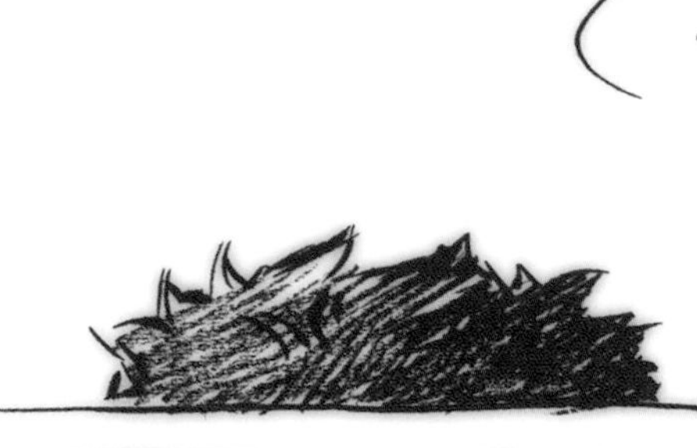
...
WHY DOES
THAT MATTER?

...

HEY!
HA HA

OH!

THANK YOU.
H-HI, NATHAN.

...

...

...I MUST'VE LOOKED PRETTY STUPID, HUH?
TRYING TO FLY.

I FORGOT... THE GRAVITY HERE IS 17 TIMES MORE THAN ON PLUTO.
SO I CAN'T.
...
...!!
...I JUST...
I MISS HOME.
SNFFLE
!!...
... DO YOU, DO YOU LIKE VIDEOGAMES?!
OR, OR MOVIES OR SOMETHING?!....

...YES!
YES, I DO!
OH, THANK GOD.
...WANT, WANT TO COME PLAY AT MY HOUSE SOMETIME?..
WHEN YOUR ARM IS BETTER...

FIN.

(in loving memory of Pluto...
we still think you are cool)

frank
and
frank

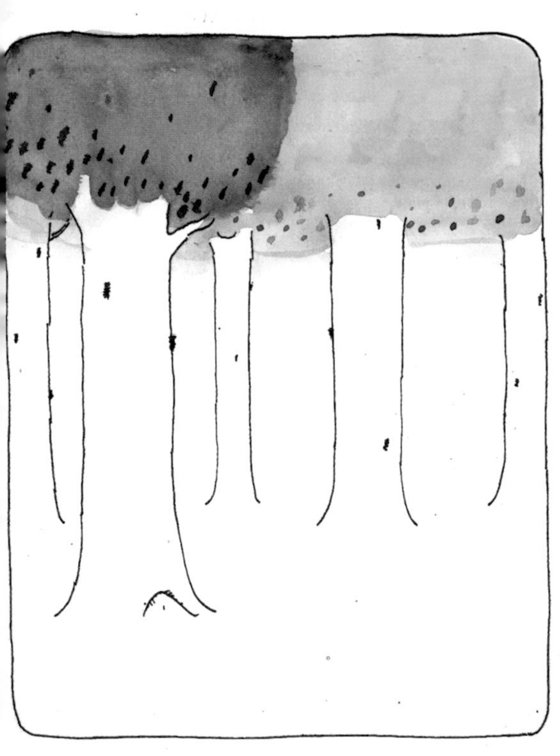

the end.

FLIGHT: VOLUME FIVE CONTRIBUTORS

JP Ahonen is a Finnish comic artist and illustrator. He couldn't have finished "Worry Dolls" without the help of his lovely fiancé, Marjaana, to whom he now owes a back rub. www.jpahonen.com; www.dailyhero.net

Graham Annable is the creator of *Grickle.* He resides in Portland, Oregon. www.grickle.com

Chris Appelhans is a freelance illustrator/ concept artist working in Alhambra, California. He shares a studio with Kazu and Phil. His work can be seen in various films and games, including the recent feature film *Monster House.*

Bannister and **Grimaldi** professionally make comics and live together in France, near a lake surrounded by mountains. They do enjoy this way of life. www.bannister.fr

Matthew Bernier is fighting to make it in the unforgiving city of Portland, Oregon. He's working on a large book for First Second, and depending on when you're reading this, it will either be a long while before it comes out, it is out right now, or it has been out for quite awhile. www.Matthew-Bernier.com.

Scott Campbell is co-founder and regular contributor to the comic anthology *Hickee.* He also does a daily online comic at www.doublefine.com called *The Double Fine Action Comics,* which is where he was art director on the video game Psychonauts. His watercolor paintings can be seen online. scott-c.blogspot.com

Svetlana Chmakova was born and raised Russian and is now Canadian, eh. She is the author of the Eisner-nominated manga series *Dramacon.* www.svetlania.com

Tony Cliff is an animator in Vancouver, British Columbia. He has also written *Delilah Dir* *and the Treasure of Constantinople,* the story o how Delilah meets Selim and rescues him fro servitude (in an adventuresome fashion). It is available through his website. www.tonycliff.co

Phil Craven is from Georgia and now lives in Southern California, where he draws comics and storyboards, and eats cereal, and kicks soc cer balls, and dreams of updating his website. www.philcraven.com

Michel Gagné was born in Québec, Canada, and has had a highly successful career drawing characters and special effects for animated and live-action feature films such as *The Iron Gian* and *Osmosis Jones.* His independant short film *Prelude to Eden* is a favorite among animation students and teachers and has played in festivals throughout the world. Michel and his wife created Gagné International Press in 1998, and he has been writing, illustrating, and publishing books and comics ever since. www.gagneint.com

Steve Hamaker is the colorist of *Bone* by day and the creator of *Fish N Chips* comics by night. http://stevehamaker.blogspot.com

Kazu Kibuishi is the editor and art director of the *Flight* comics anthology. He has also written and illustrated the graphic novels *Amulet* and *Daisy Kutter.* His webcomic *Copper* can b found at his website. www.boltcity.com

Kness and **Made** are both freelance illustrator based in Paris. Founders of the digital creative community www.cfsl.net, they are working on their second collective art book. www..kness.ne www.m4de.com

onny Liew is a Eisner-nominated artist whose ork includes *My Faith in Frankie, Re-Gifters, Vonderland,* and the Xeric Award–winning *Aalinky Robot.* He is currently putting together n anthology called *Liquid City.* www.sonny ew.com

Reagan Lodge is a sequential art mercenary, orever wandering in search of glory and adenture. He has worked as a concept artist in e tactical body armor industry and as a comic rtist for Nickelodeon's magazine. www.reagan odge.com

s a child, **John Martz** spent most of his time rawing cartoons, reading books, and living in motionally unhealthy fantasy worlds. As an dult, he is somewhat hairier. He works as an lustrator from his home in Toronto, where he lso runs the illustration and cartooning blog *Drawn!* www.johnmartz.com; www.drawn.ca

arah Mensinga lives in Texas with her usband. After several years working in the nimation industry as an animator and designer, he is now writing a graphic novel. www.sarah nensinga.com

Ryan North is a cartoonist living in Toronto, Canada. He creates *Dinosaur Comics,* a free nline strip, which can be read at www.qwantz com. He is a very tall man, but he wears it vell.

Richard Pose is a storyboard artist at Titmouse, nc. His credits include *Metalocalypse* and *Happy Monster Band.* He wants to thank his riends Mike, Israel, Josh, Ryan, Matt, and ustin for their help coloring "Béisbol 2." www.richardpose.com. PS: He loves baseball.

Paul Rivoche is an illustrator, designer, and omic book artist who has written and illusrated comics for Adhouse Books' acclaimed *Project* series of anthologies, drawn stories nd covers for DC Comics, and done key ackground designs for many WB Animation rojects, including *Batman, Batman Beyond, uperman,* and the recent *Justice League: New Frontier* DVD. www.rocketfiction.blogspot.com

Dave Roman draws a webcomic called *Astronaut Elementary* and has collaborated on everal books, including *Jax Epoch, Adventures of Tymm,* and *Agnes Quill.* He'd like to thank his friends Alison, Alisa, Colleen, Jamie, Lisa, Naseem, and Shelli for helping him finish coloring his story on time! www.yaytime.com

Israel Sanchez studied art at Cal State Fullerton and now works as a freelance illustrator in La Habra, California. www.israelsanchez.com

Kean Soo writes and draws *Jellaby* from his fortress of solitude in the frozen north. His second Jellaby graphic novel will be released in early 2009. www.secretfriendsociety.com

Joey Weiser has contributed to several comics anthologies, including past and present volumes of *Flight.* His first graphic novel, *The Ride Home,* was published in 2007 by AdHouse Books. He lives with his girlfriend, Michele, and their timecat, Eddie. www.tragic-planet.com